COLUMBIA UNIVERSITY
INDO-IRANIAN SERIES

EDITED BY

A. V. WILLIAMS JACKSON

PROFESSOR OF INDO-IRANIAN LANGUAGES
IN COLUMBIA UNIVERSITY

Volume Eleven

THE ZOROASTRIAN DOCTRINE
OF A FUTURE LIFE

BY

JAL DASTUR CURSETJI PAVRY

THE ZOROASTRIAN DOCTRINE OF A FUTURE LIFE

FROM DEATH TO THE INDIVIDUAL JUDGMENT

BY

JAL DASTUR CURSETJI PAVRY, A.M., Ph.D.

LATE FELLOW OF MULLA FIROZ MADRESSA AND OF ST. XAVIER'S COLLEGE,
BOMBAY UNIVERSITY; SOMETIME FELLOW AND LECTURER IN
INDO-IRANIAN LANGUAGES, COLUMBIA UNIVERSITY

Second Edition

AMS PRESS INC.
NEW YORK
1965

Copyright 1926, 1929, Columbia University Press, New York

Reprinted with Permission of the

Original Publisher, 1965

AMS PRESS INC.

New York, N. Y. 10003

Manufactured in the United States of America

TO
MY FATHER
AND
TO THE MEMORY OF
MY MOTHER

PREFACE TO THE SECOND EDITION

The kind reception given to my book has encouraged me to republish it, and in order that it may prove of still greater use to students of religion, and, in particular, to specialists in the field of Iranian research, I have appended, in addition to the general index, two important indexes: Index of Passages Translated, and Index of Pahlavi Words. Some new material, moreover, has been incorporated in a few of the footnotes,[1] the text of the first edition being reproduced without alterations.

As noted in my preface to the first edition, the present work is the first of three separate monographs, in which I propose to treat of the Zoroastrian doctrine of a future life in its three phases, namely, the period from death to the Individual Judgment at the Chinvat Bridge (*judicium particulare*), life in Heaven, Hell, or the Intermediate Place, and the General Judgment (*judicium universale*). Relevant passages from the Gāthic and the Later Avestan texts, the Pahlavi and the Parsi-Persian writings are translated by the author with critical notes, most of the extracts from the Parsi-Persian literature being translated here for the first time.

Since the publication of this book in 1926, there has appeared a monumental work on Zoroastrianism: *Iranian Studies*, by my revered father, Dastur Cursetji Erachji Pavry. I should like to call the special attention of my readers to this book,[2] and also to my recent publication in Gujarati, entitled *Yasht e Vadardegān*, which deals with the Zoroastrian Sacraments and Ordinances, with special reference to the prayers and ceremonies for the dying and the dead.

JAL DASTUR CURSETJI PAVRY.

LONDON,
June 21, 1928.

[1] See p. 16, n. 33, 34; p. 26, n. 19; p. 28, n. 1; p. 77, n. 19; p. 86, n. 76; p. 90, n. 104; p. 103, n. 20, 21. It may be noted here that in introducing the new material particular care has been taken not to alter the original pagination.

[2] See particularly Chapter 10 (= pages 168–193), which treats of the 'Ceremonials connected with the Dead.'

PREFACE TO THE FIRST EDITION

The doctrine of a life eternal for the immortal soul and the ultimate regeneration of the world when all things shall have come to an end is one of the striking features in Zarathushtra's teachings which have commanded the attention of students of religion, and the subject has often been dealt with. There would seem to be room, however, for a new presentation which should collect and co-ordinate the material from every period of Zoroastrianism in the light both of its age-long tradition and of the most recent Iranian research; and this is the fundamental purpose of the task I have here undertaken. The present monograph, accordingly, is the result of a careful study of all the relevant passages in the Gāthic and the Later Avestan texts, which I have translated [1] with critical notes; and these I have supplemented by comprehensive researches in the Pahlavi books, to which I have given particular attention. I may add that it has perhaps been possible to develop certain additional aspects in the light of modern Parsi beliefs and observances with which Western scholars may not be so familiar.

Since my object has been to present the doctrine of a future life primarily as a tenet of the Zoroastrian religion, I have been compelled to refrain from calling attention to the resemblances that exist between the eschatological ideas in Zoroastrianism and those of other faiths, notably Judaism and Christianity, and also from dealing with the possibility of mutual influences. To have done this would have increased the size of the book unduly. Besides, there exist two excellent monographs on this particular phase of the subject: Söderblom's *La Vie future d'après le mazdéisme* and Böklen's *Die Verwandtschaft der jüdisch-*

[1] For obvious reasons, I have made my translations very literal, often at the expense of style.

christlichen mit der Parsischen Eschatologie.[2] Nor has the scope of the present monograph allowed me to discuss the possible eschatological ideas of the Iranian people before Zarathushtra, much less those of the Indo-Iranian and other Indo-European groups. I have noted, however, certain parallels to be found in Manichaeism, on account of its especially close relation with Zoroastrianism, and because I have already dealt with this topic in my Essay for the degree of Master of Arts at Columbia University (February, 1922), entitled *Manichaeism and Zoroastrian Influence upon the Manichaean Doctrine of Eschatology.*

The subject divides itself naturally into three parts. The present work carries the investigation only through the immediate fate and judgment of the individual soul at the Chinvat Bridge (the *judicium particulare*), leaving the topics of the future state in Heaven, Hell, or the Intermediate Place, and of the General Judgment (*judicium universale*), for which I have the material in hand, to be treated later in succeeding parts of the work. The trilogy, the present writer hopes, will set forth in a systematic way the Zoroastrian doctrine of a future life, as enunciated throughout the entire Zoroastrian literature from the old Avestan Gāthās to the latest Parsi religious writings.

In the present work I have arranged the material topically, taking up under each head the sources (Gāthās, Later Avesta, Pahlavi, Parsi-Persian) in chronological order; but the introductory chapter presents a view of the various periods of Zoroastrian literature in their special relation to the theme, and the conclusion sketches in brief outline the doctrine as a whole.

Before closing these prefatory remarks, I desire to express the deep debt of gratitude I owe to friends. I wish to thank Professor Louis H. Gray, of the University of Nebraska, and Dr. Charles J. Ogden, of Columbia University, who kindly volunteered to go through the manuscript and who have made many valuable suggestions in the final revision of the book. To Dr.

[2] See the General Bibliography for these and other related works on the subject.

Ogden, who has very generously devoted much time to the improvement of the manuscript, my thanks are especially due.

I also wish to express my obligations to Dr. Ogden, to Professor Clarence A. Manning, of Columbia University, and particularly to Dr. George C. O. Haas, sometime Fellow in Indo-Iranian Languages at Columbia University, for their kindness in going over the proofsheets as they came from the press. Dr. Haas has also very kindly placed at my disposal his wide knowledge and great technical skill in all matters relating to the make-up of the volume.

And I wish to record here, above all, some expression, however inadequate, of the debt of thanks I owe to my friend and teacher, Professor A. V. Williams Jackson, whose profound learning and sound scholarship have been an unfailing source of inspiration. It is under his able tutelage that I have spent four of the happiest and most instructive years of my life. To the knowledge which he has imparted so freely and so abundantly and to his devoted zeal and interest I ascribe all that may be best in my work. My years of association with him at Columbia, as pupil and as co-worker, will ever remain a happy memory.

JAL DASTUR CURSETJI PAVRY.

COLUMBIA UNIVERSITY,
December 28, 1925.

CONTENTS

PREFACE TO THE SECOND EDITION vii
PREFACE TO THE FIRST EDITION viii
NOTE ON THE TRANSCRIPTION OF IRANIAN WORDS. . . xiv
ABBREVIATIONS AND SYMBOLS xv
BIBLIOGRAPHY xviii
    A. Editions and translations of texts xviii
        1. Avestan xviii
        2. Pahlavi xix
        3. Parsi-Persian xxii
    B. Works of reference xxii
    C. General bibliography xxiii

CHAPTER I. INTRODUCTION 1
Zarathushtra's message of immortality 1
The sources in general 2
The Gāthās 4
The Later Avesta 5
The Pahlavi literature 6
The Parsi-Persian writings 7
Present-day ceremonies 8

CHAPTER II. THE SOUL OF THE RIGHTEOUS DURING THE
    FIRST THREE NIGHTS AFTER DEATH 9
Introduction 9
The soul of the righteous in the Later Avesta . . . 9
The soul of the righteous in Pahlavi literature . . . 12
The soul of the righteous in Parsi-Persian literature . . 18

CHAPTER III. THE SOUL OF THE WICKED DURING THE
    FIRST THREE NIGHTS AFTER DEATH 21
The soul of the wicked in the Later Avesta . . . 21

The soul of the wicked in Pahlavi literature 23
The soul of the wicked in Parsi-Persian literature. . . . 26

CHAPTER IV. THE MANIFESTATION OF THE DAĒNĀ, OR
    CONSCIENCE, TO THE SOUL, ACCORDING TO THE GĀTHĀS. 28
    Introduction: discussion of the term Daēnā 28
    The office of the Daēnā in the Gāthās 29

CHAPTER V. THE MANIFESTATION OF THE DAĒNĀ, OR
    CONSCIENCE, TO THE SOUL, ACCORDING TO THE LATER
    AVESTA 33
    Introduction 33
    The Daēnā greets the soul of the righteous. 33
    The Daēnā meets the soul of the wicked 37

CHAPTER VI. THE MANIFESTATION OF THE DAĒNĀ, OR
    CONSCIENCE, TO THE SOUL, ACCORDING TO THE PAHLAVI
    AND PARSI-PERSIAN LITERATURE. 39
    The Daēnā greets the righteous soul 39
    The Daēnā meets the wicked soul 41
    The Daēnā in the Parsi-Persian literature 44
ADDENDUM: ON THE FIGURES THAT MEET THE SOUL IN
    MANICHAEISM 46

CHAPTER VII. THE INDIVIDUAL JUDGMENT ACCORDING
    TO THE GĀTHĀS. 49
    Introduction 49
    The store of Good Works, and their accounting . . . 49
    The Judgment at the Chinvat Bridge 53
    The Judges at the assize 56
    Conclusion 59

CHAPTER VIII. THE INDIVIDUAL JUDGMENT ACCORDING
    TO THE LATER AVESTA. 60
    Introduction 60
    The store of Good Works recorded 60
    The Judgment as described in the Vidēvdāt 62

The triad of heavenly Judges.	67
The struggle between the Powers of Good and Evil at the Judgment.	69
The important role played by the Chinvat Bridge in the Later Avesta.	69
Conclusion.	71

CHAPTER IX. THE INDIVIDUAL JUDGMENT ACCORDING TO THE PAHLAVI WRITINGS. 72

Introduction	72
The store of Good Works.	72
The Treasure-house of Perpetual Profit.	74
Repentance and expiation.	77
The five indispensable Good Works.	78
The Chinvat Bridge and its location.	79
The Judgment at the Chinvat Bridge: the reckoning and the weighing.	80
The passage of the soul over the Chinvat Bridge.	91
Conclusion.	97

CHAPTER X. THE INDIVIDUAL JUDGMENT ACCORDING TO THE PARSI-PERSIAN LITERATURE. 99

Introduction	99
The store of Good Works, and related ideas	99
The soul at the Chinvat Bridge	101
Passage of the soul over the Chinvat Bridge	105
Conclusion.	111

CHAPTER XI. CONCLUSION. 112

INDEXES 115

NOTE ON THE TRANSCRIPTION OF IRANIAN WORDS

The system here adopted for the scientific transliteration of Avestan, Pahlavi, and Modern Persian words is substantially that employed by various scholars in the *Grundriss der iranischen Philologie* and in particular by Bartholomae in his *Altiranisches Wörterbuch* (see especially his introduction, page 23).

This exact mode of transcription is used to represent Iranian words when quoted from the texts translated by the author or when adduced in the footnotes. In these cases the words are printed in italics. In order to facilitate pronunciation, a slightly different method of transcription is followed when Iranian proper names and titles of books occur in continuous English text and are printed in roman type (*š* being represented by *sh*, *č* by *ch*, etc.).

Two points are particularly to be noted in connection with the transliteration of Pahlavi. First, the titles of Pahlavi works are uniformly given in the old Pahlavi form rather than in a form inclining to Modern Persian (e.g. *Vičarkart i Dēnīk* instead of *Vijirkard i Dēnīg*). Secondly, the Huzvārish words occurring in the Pahlavi text are invariably replaced (in accordance with the principles enunciated by Bartholomae in *Indogermanische Forschungen*, vol. 38, page 39) by the Pāzand equivalents which those word-forms were intended to represent.

ABBREVIATIONS AND SYMBOLS

AF.	*Arische Forschungen* (Bartholomae).
AirWb.	*Altiranisches Wörterbuch* (Bartholomae).
Aog.	Aogemadaēchā.
Av.	Avesta, Avestan.
AV.	Arda Viraf (in titles of books); cf. AVN.
AVN.	Artāk Vīrāz Nāmak.
A.Y.	(*Anno Yazdakart*); Yazdagardian era.
BB.	*Bezzenberger's Beiträge zur Kunde der indogermanischen Sprachen.*
Bd.	Bundahishn (Indian recension).
Bh.	Behistan inscription of Darius.
bk.	book.
BSOS.	*Bulletin of the School of Oriental Studies, London Institution.*
Bthl.	Bartholomae (Prof. Dr. Christian).
comm.	commentary.
DD.	Dātastān i Dēnīk.
Dk.	Dēnkart.
Enc. Brit.	*Encyclopaedia Britannica.*
ERE.	*Encyclopaedia of Religion and Ethics*, ed. Hastings.
Ét. ir.	*Études iraniennes* (Darmesteter).
EZ.	*Early Zoroastrianism* (Moulton).
Frag.	Fragment.
GIrPh.	*Grundriss der iranischen Philologie.*
GS.	Ganj i Shāhīkān.
HAM.	Handarz i Āturpāt i Mahraspandān.
Hdt.	Herodotus.
HHK.	Handarz i Hōsrav i Kavātān.
HN.	Hadhōkht Nask.
ibid.	(*ibidem*); in the same work.
IF.	*Indogermanische Forschungen.*

IrBd.	Iranian Bundahishn.
JA.	*Journal Asiatique.*
JAOS.	*Journal of the American Oriental Society.*
JBBRAS.	*Journal of the Bombay Branch of the Royal Asiatic Society.*
LAv.	Later Avesta.
MX.	Dātastān i Mēnūk i Khrat.
n.d.	no date.
Ner.	Neryosangh.
Nīr.	Nīrangastān.
NP.	New Persian.
Ny.	Nyāishes.
op. cit.	(*opus citatum*); the work previously cited.
Pāz.	Pāzend.
Phl.	Pahlavi.
PhlHN.	Pahlavi Hadhōkht Nask.
PhlRiv.	Pahlavi Rivāyat.
PhlVd.	Pahlavi Vidēvdāt (Vendīdād).
Phl. vers.	Pahlavi version.
RivDH.	Rivāyat of Dārāb Hormazdyār.
SBE.	*Sacred Books of the East.*
SD.	Sad Dar.
SDBd.	Sad Dar Bundahish.
Skt.	Sanskrit.
ŠNŠ.	Shāyist nē-Shāyist.
ŠVV.	Shkand-vimānīk Vichār.
Sr.	Sīrōchak.
TPhl.	Turfan Pahlavi.
vb.	verb.
Vd.	Vidēvdāt (Vendīdād).
vers.	version.
Vr.	Visprat.
VYt.	Vishtāsp Yasht.
VZsp.	Vichītakīhā i Zātsparam.
WFr.	Westergaard Fragment.

WZKM.	*Wiener Zeitschrift für die Kunde des Morgenlandes.*
Ys.	Yasna.
Yt.	Yasht.
ZA.	*Le Zend Avesta* (Darmesteter).
ZDMG.	*Zeitschrift der Deutschen Morgenländischen Gesellschaft.*
< >	indicate glosses or explanations in the original text.
[ ]	indicate words inserted by the present writer to supply omissions in the original text.
( )	indicate words and phrases inserted by the present writer to round out the grammatical structure of the English translation or to make clear the sense.

BIBLIOGRAPHY

A. EDITIONS AND TRANSLATIONS OF TEXTS.

1. AVESTAN.

Avesta. Avesta, die heiligen Schriften der Parsen . . . im Grundtexte sammt der Huzvâresch-Übersetzung herausgegeben von Dr. Friedrich Spiegel. 2 vols., Vienna, 1853, 1858.

   Still valuable for the Pahlavi version.

—— Zendavesta, or the Religious Books of the Zoroastrians, edited by N. L. Westergaard. Vol. I, The Zend Texts. Copenhagen, 1852–1854.

   Still important for the Fragments, such as the Hadhōkht Nask and Vishtāsp Yasht.

—— Avesta, the Sacred Books of the Parsis, edited by Karl F. Geldner. 3 vols., Stuttgart, 1886–1896.

—— Collected Sanskrit Writings of the Parsis, edited by Sheriarji Dadabhai Bharucha. Part I, Khorda-Avestâ-Arthaḥ, Bombay, 1906; part II, Ijisni [Yasna], Bombay, 1910.

   Contains the Sanskrit version of Neryosangh.

—— The Zend-Avesta, Part I: The Vendîdâd, translated by James Darmesteter. 2d edition, Oxford, 1895. (*SBE.* vol. 4.)

—— The Zend-Avesta, Part II: The Sîrôzahs, Yasts, and Nyâyis, translated by James Darmesteter. Oxford, 1883. (*SBE.* vol. 23.)

   Contains a translation of the Hadhōkht Nask and Vishtāsp Yasht.

—— The Zend-Avesta, Part III: The Yasna, Visparad, Âfrînagân, Gâhs, and Miscellaneous Fragments, translated by L. H. Mills. Oxford, 1887. (*SBE.* vol. 31.)

—— Le Zend-Avesta. Traduction nouvelle avec commentaire historique et philologique, par James Darmesteter. 3 vols.,

Paris, 1892–1893. (*Annales du Musée Guimet*, vols. 21, 22, 24.)

—— Avesta, die heiligen Bücher der Parsen, übersetzt auf der Grundlage von Chr. Bartholomae's Altiranischem Wörterbuch, von Fritz Wolff. Strassburg, 1910.

<small>Does not contain the Gāthās, which had been previously translated by Bartholomae (see below).</small>

—— Extracts translated by Karl F. Geldner in *Religionsgeschichtliches Lesebuch*, ed. A. Bertholet, p. 323–360, Tübingen, 1908.

<small>See especially pages 351–359, 'Tod und Jenseits.'</small>

The Gāthās. Die Gatha's des Awesta. Zarathustra's Verspredigten, übersetzt von Christian Bartholomae. Strassburg, 1905.

—— A Hymn of Zoroaster: Yasna 31, translated with Comments by A. V. Williams Jackson. Stuttgart, 1888.

—— Translated by J. H. Moulton, in his *Early Zoroastrianism*, p. 343–390, London, 1913.

Hadhōkht Nask. Edited and translated by Martin Haug; see under Artāk Vīrāz Nāmak, below.

Vidēvdāt. Vendidâd: Avesta Text with Pahlavi Translation and Commentary, and Glossarial Index. Edited by Dastoor Hoshang Jamasp. 2 vols., Bombay, 1907.

2. PAHLAVI.

Aogemadaēchā. Aogemadaêcâ, ein Pârsentractat in Pâzend, Altbaktrisch und Sanskrit, herausgegeben, übersetzt, erklärt und mit Glossar versehen von Dr. Wilhelm Geiger. Erlangen, 1878.

—— Translated by Darmesteter in *SBE*. vol. 4 (2d ed.), p. 372–386.

Artāk Vīrāz Nāmak. Arda Viraf Nameh: The original Pahlavi text, with an introduction, notes, Gujarati translation, and Persian version of Zartosht Bahram in verse, by Kaikhusru Dastur Jamaspji Jamasp Asa. Bombay, 1902.

—— The Book of Arda Viraf, . . . Gosht-i Fryano, and Hadokht-Nask, edited and translated by Hoshangji Jamaspji Asa, Martin Haug, and E. W. West. Bombay and London, 1872.

Avesta (Pahlavi version). Edited by F. Spiegel in his edition of the Avesta (see above).

Bundahishn (Iranian). The Bûndahishn, being a Facsimile of the TD MS. No. 2, brought from Persia by Dastur Tîrandâz and now preserved in the late Ervad Tahmuras' Library. Edited by Behramgore Tahmuras Anklesaria. Bombay, 1908. (The Pahlavi Text Series, vol. 3.)

—— An Untranslated Chapter of the Bundehesh, by J. J. Modi. In *Journal of the Bombay Branch of the Royal Asiatic Society*, 21. 49–65. [Reprinted in his *Asiatic Papers*, 1. 217–234, Bombay, 1905.]

Text and translation of chapter 30.

Bundahishn (Indian). The Bundahis. Translated by E. W. West, in *Pahlavi Texts*, Part 1, p. 1–151, Oxford, 1880 (*SBE.* vol. 5).

Dātastān i Dēnīk. The Datistan-i Dinik, Pahlavi Text containing 92 Questions, asked by Mitr-Khurshit Atur-Mahan and others, to Manush-Chihar Goshn-Jam, Leader of the Zoroastrians in Persia, about 881 A.D., and their Answers, ed. Tahmuras Dinshaji Anklesaria. Part I, Pursishn I–XL, Bombay, n. d.

—— Dâdistân-î Dînîk. Translated by E. W. West, in *Pahlavi Texts*, Part 2, p. 1–276, Oxford, 1882 (*SBE.* vol. 18).

The references to chapters and sections in the present volume follow the numbering of West's translation.

Dātastān i Mēnūk i Khrat. Dânâku Mainyô-i Khard: Pahlavi, Pazand, and Sanskrit Texts, edited by T. D. Anklesaria. Bombay, 1913.

—— Dînâ-î Maînôg-î Khirad. Translated by E. W. West, in *Pahlavi Texts*, Part 3, p. 1–113, Oxford, 1885 (*SBE.* vol. 24).

Dēnkart. The Dinkard, edited and translated by P. B. and D. P. Sanjana. Vols. 1–18, Bombay, 1874–1926.

—— The Complete Text of the Pahlavi Dinkard, published by Dhanjishah Meherjibhai Madan. 2 vols., Bombay, 1911.

—— Translated by E. W. West: books 8 and 9 in *Pahlavi Texts*, Part 4, Oxford, 1891 (*SBE.* vol. 37); books 7 and 5. 1–4, *ibid.*, Part 5, p. 3–130, Oxford, 1897 (*SBE.* vol. 47).

The references to chapters and sections of books 7, 8, and 9 follow the numbering of West's translation.

Ganj i Shāhīkān, Handarz i Āturpāt i Mahraspandān, Handarz i Hōsrav i Kavātān. Ganjesháyagán, Andarze Átrepát Máráspandán, Mádigáne Chatrang, and Andarze Khusroe Kavátán, edited and translated by Peshutan Dastur Behramji Sanjana. Bombay, 1885.

Mēnūk i Khrat, see Dātastān i Mēnūk i Khrat.

Nīrangastān. Nirangistan. A photozincographed Facsimile of a MS. belonging to Shams-ul-Ulama Dastur Dr. Hoshangjee Jamaspjee of Poona, edited with an Introduction and Collation with an Older Iranian MS. in the Possession of Ervad Tahmuras D. Anklesaria, by Darab Dastur Peshotan Sanjana. London, 1894.

—— Aêrpatastân and Nîrangastân, or the Code of the Holy Doctorship and the Code of the Divine Service, being Portions of the great Husparam Nask, on the Order, the Ministry, the Officiation, and the Equipment of the Holy Divines of the Noble Zarathushtrian Church. Translated by Sohrab Jamshedjee Bulsara. Bombay, 1915.

Pahlavi Rivāyat. The Pahlavi Rivâyat accompanying the Dâdistân-î Dînîk. Edited by B. N. Dhabhar. Bombay, 1913.

Pahlavi version of the Avesta, see Avesta, editions of Spiegel and Hoshang Jamasp, above.

Pāzend writings. Pâzend Texts, collected and collated by Edalji Kersâspji Antiâ. Bombay, 1909.

Shāyist nē-Shāyist. Shâyast lâ-shâyast. Translated by E. W.

West, in *Pahlavi Texts*, Part 1, p. 237-406, Oxford, 1880 (*SBE.* vol. 5).

Shkand-vimānīk Vichār. Shikand-Gûmânîk Vijâr: the Pazand-Sanskrit Text together with a Fragment of the Pahlavi, ed. Hôshang Dastûr Jâmâspji Jâmâsp-Âsânâ and E. W. West. Bombay, 1887.

—— *S*ikand-gûmânîk Vigâr. Translated by E. W. West, in *Pahlavi Texts*, Part 3, p. 115-251, Oxford, 1885 (*SBE.* vol. 24).

Vichītakīhā i Zātsparam. Selections of Zâ*d*-sparam. Translated by E. W. West: part 1, chapters 1-11, in *Pahlavi Texts*, Part 1, p. 153-187, Oxford, 1880 (*SBE.* vol. 5); part 1, chapters 12-24, *ibid.*, Part 5, p. 133-170, Oxford, 1897 (*SBE.* vol. 47).

3. PARSI-PERSIAN.

Rivāyat i Dārāb Hormazdyār. Dârâb Hormazyâr's Rivâyat. Ed. by Manockji Rustamji Unvâlâ. 2 vols., Bombay, 1922.

—— Rivāyate Dastur Dārāb Hamjiar. (Gujarati Version.) Ed. R. J. Dastur Meherji Rana. Navsari, 1896.

Sad Dar. Saddar Naṣr. Ed. by B. N. Dhabhar. Bombay, 1909.

—— Sad Dar. Translated by E. W. West, in *Pahlavi Texts*, Part 3, p. 253-361, Oxford, 1885 (*SBE.* vol. 24).

Sad Dar Bundahish. Saddar Bundehesh. Edited by B. N. Dhabhar. Bombay, 1909.

In one volume with Saddar Naṣr (see above).

B. WORKS OF REFERENCE.

Bartholomae, Chr. Awestasprache und Altpersisch. In *GIrPh*. 1. 1. 152-248.

—— Altiranisches Wörterbuch. Strassburg, 1904.

—— Zum altiranischen Wörterbuch: Nacharbeiten und Vorarbeiten. Strassburg, 1906. (*IF.* vol. 19, Beiheft.)

Clemen, C. Fontes Historiae Religionis Persicae. Bonn, 1920.

Geldner, Karl F. Awestalitteratur. In *GIrPh*. 2. 1-53.

Horn, Paul. Grundriss der neupersischen Etymologie. Strassburg, 1893. (*Sammlung Indogermanischer Wörterbücher*, vol. 4.)

Hübschmann, H. Persische Studien. Strassburg, 1895.

Jackson, A. V. Williams. An Avesta Grammar, in Comparison with Sanskrit. Part I. Stuttgart, 1892.

Part II, dealing with the syntax, has never been published.

—— Avesta Reader. First Series. Stuttgart, 1893.

Junker, Heinrich F. J. The Frahang i Pahlavīk. Heidelberg, 1912.

Reichelt, Hans. Awestisches Elementarbuch. Heidelberg, 1909.

—— Avesta Reader. Texts, Notes, Glossary and Index. Strassburg, 1911.

—— Der Frahang i oīm. In *Wiener Zeitschrift für die Kunde des Morgenlandes*, 14. 177–213 and 15. 117–186 (1900, 1901).

Salemann, C. Mittelpersisch. In *GIrPh*. 1. 1. 249–332.

Steingass, F. Persian-English Dictionary. London, n. d.

West, E. W. Pahlavi Literature. In *GIrPh*. 2. 75–129.

C. GENERAL BIBLIOGRAPHY.

Ayuso, F. G. Los Pueblos iranios y Zoroastro. Madrid, 1874. Pages 168–186.

This Spanish presentation is based on Haug's *Essays* (see below), and has no value as an independent work.

Bertholet, Alfred. Zur Frage des Verhältnisses von persischem und jüdischem Auferstehungsglauben. In *Festschrift F. C. Andreas*, p. 51–62, Leipzig, 1916.

Böklen, Ernst. Die Verwandtschaft der jüdisch-christlichen mit der Parsischen Eschatologie. Göttingen, 1902.

Bousset, W. Die Himmelsreise der Seele: Die Vorstellungen auf dem Gebiet der eranischen Religion. In *Archiv für Religionswissenschaft*, 4 (1901), p. 155–169.

Brandt, W. Das Schicksal der Seele nach dem Tode nach mandäischen und parsischen Vorstellungen. In *Jahrbücher für protestantische Theologie*, 18 (1892), p. 405–438, 575–603.

Casartelli, L. C. La Philosophie religieuse du mazdéisme sous les Sassanides. Louvain, 1884.

—— The Philosophy of the Mazdayasnian Religion under the Sassanids. Translated from the French by Firoz Jamaspji J. Jamasp Asa. Bombay, 1889.

<small>An English translation of the preceding.</small>

—— Avestan *Urvan*, "Soul." In *A Volume of Oriental Studies presented to E. G. Browne*, ed. by T. W. Arnold and R. A. Nicholson, p. 127–128, Cambridge, 1922.

—— Article 'Salvation (Iranian).' In *ERE*. 11. 137–138.

—— Article 'Sin (Iranian).' In *ERE*. 11. 562–566.

—— Article 'State of the Dead (Iranian).' In *ERE*. 11. 847–849.

Clemen, Carl. Die griechischen und lateinischen Nachrichten über die persische Religion. Giessen, 1920.

Darmesteter, James. Études iraniennes. 2 vols., Paris, 1882, 1883. Vol. 2, pages 206–208.

Dhalla, M. N. Zoroastrian Theology. New York, privately printed, 1914.

Geiger, Wilhelm. Ostirānische Kultur im Altertum. Erlangen, 1882. Pages 273–286. [English translation by Darab Dastur Peshotan Sanjana, 2 vols., London, 1885–1886; vol. 1, pages 96–111.]

Geldner, Karl F. Article 'Zoroaster.' In *Encyclopaedia Britannica*, 11th ed., vol. 28, p. 1039–1043.

Gorvala, R. F. The Immortal Soul. In *Spiegel Memorial Volume*, p. 99–124, Bombay, 1908.

Gray, Louis H. Article 'Life and Death (Iranian).' In *ERE*. 8. 37.

—— Zoroastrian Elements in Muhammedan Eschatology. In *Le Muséon*, new series, vol. 3, p. 153–184, Louvain, 1902.

Haas, George C. O. An Avestan Fragment on the Resurrection (Fr. W. 4), edited with Translation and Notes. In *Spiegel Memorial Volume*, p. 181–187, Bombay, 1908.

Haug, M. Essays on the Sacred Language, Writings and Religion of the Parsis. Third edition, edited and enlarged by E. W. West. London, 1884. Pages 310–314.

Henry, V. Le Parsisme. Paris, 1905. Pages 197–213.

Hübschmann, H. Die parsische Lehre vom Jenseits und jüngsten Gericht. In *Jahrbücher für prot. Theologie*, vol. 5 (1879), p. 203–245.

Jackson, A. V. Williams. Die iranische Religion. In *GIrPh*. 2. 612–708, Strassburg, 1903. Pages 683–687.

—— A New Reference in the Avesta to the 'Life-book' hereafter. In *JAOS*. 14, Proceedings, p. 20–21 (1888).

—— Weighing the Soul in the Balance after Death, an Indian as well as Iranian Idea. In *Actes du Dixième Congrès International des Orientalistes* (*Session de Genève*, 1894), part 2, Leiden, 1895, p. 65–74.

—— Avestan *ayōkhšusta* 'molten metal,' *ayah*, and its Significance in the Gāthās. In *JAOS*. 15, Proceedings, p. 58–61 (1890).

—— The Ancient Persian Conception of Salvation according to the Avesta, or Bible of Zoroaster. In *American Journal of Theology*, 17. 195–205, April, 1913.

—— The Doctrine of the Resurrection among the Ancient Persians. In *JAOS*. 16, Proceedings, p. 38–39 (1893).

—— The Ancient Persian Doctrine of a Future Life. In *Religion and the Future Life*, ed. by E. Hershey Sneath, p. 121–140, New York, 1922.

> Reproduces, with additions and changes, the material of an address made at the opening of the Haskell Oriental Museum of the University of Chicago in 1896; see *The Biblical World*, 8. 149–163, Chicago, 1896.

Justi, F. Himmel und Hölle der Parsen. In *Münchener Allgemeine Zeitung*, Beilage, 1888, p. 4625–4626.

Kohut, A. Was hat die talmudische Eschatologie aus dem Parsismus aufgenommen? In *ZDMG*. 21 (1867), p. 552–591.

Lehmann, E. Zarathustra: en Bog om Persernes gamle Tro.

2 vols., Copenhagen, 1899, 1902. Volume 2, pages 107–126 and 250–266.

—— Die Perser. In *Lehrbuch der Religionsgeschichte*, ed. P. D. Chantepie de la Saussaye, 3d ed., vol. 2, p. 162–233, Tübingen, 1905.

See especially pages 218–226: 'Tod und Jenseits. Die letzten Dinge.'

MacCulloch, J. A. Article 'Eschatology.' In *ERE*. 5. 373–391.

Cf. esp. page 376 (Parsi).

Meillet, A. Trois Conférences sur les Gâthâ de l'Avesta. Paris, 1925. (*Annales du Musée Guimet, Bibliothèque de Vulgarisation*, vol. 44.)

Meyer, Eduard. Ursprung und Anfänge des Christentums. 3 vols., Stuttgart and Berlin, 1921, 1923. Vol. 2 (1921), p. 58–94, 111–117, 174–184, 189–204.

Mills, L. H. Avesta Eschatology compared with the Books of Daniel and Revelations. Chicago, 1908.

—— Our Own Religion in Ancient Persia. Oxford, 1913. Pages 128–138.

—— Immortality in the Gâthas. In *The Thinker*, 2. 104–112, London, 1892.

Modi, Jivanji Jamshedji. The Belief about the Future of the Soul among the Ancient Egyptians and Iranians. In *JBBRAS*. 19 (1897), p. 365–374. [Reprinted in the author's *Asiatic Papers*, vol. 1, p. 137–146, Bombay, 1905.]

—— The Religious Ceremonies and Customs of the Parsees. Bombay, 1922. Pages 51–85, 361–370, 419–426, 427–428, 465–479.

Moulton, J. H. Early Zoroastrianism. London, 1913. Pages 154–181.

—— The Treasure of the Magi. London, 1917. Pages 31–49, 72–74, 104–110.

—— The Zoroastrian Conception of a Future Life. In *Journal of Transactions of the Victoria Institute*, 47. 233–252, London, 1915.

Patterson, L. Mithraism and Christianity. Cambridge, 1921. Pages 56–88.

Reitzenstein, R. Das iranische Erlösungsmysterium. Bonn, 1921.

Reuterskiöld, E. Zarathustras religionshistoriska Ställning. Upsala, 1914. Pages 189–207.

Sanjana, R. E. Dastur P. The Parsi Book of Books, the Zend-Avesta. Bombay, 1925.

> See esp. chapter 5 = pages 334–444: 'Zoroastrian eschatology.'

Scheftelowitz, I. Die altpersische Religion und das Judentum: Unterschiede, Übereinstimmungen und gegenseitige Beeinflussungen. Giessen, 1920.

> See especially chapters 15–18, pages 158–216.

Söderblom, Nathan. Article 'Death and Disposal of the Dead (Parsi).' In *ERE.* 4. 502–505.

—— La Vie future d'après le mazdéisme à la lumière des croyances parallèles dans les autres religions: étude d'eschatologie comparée. Paris, 1901. (*Annales du Musée Guimet, Bibliothèque d'Études*, vol. 9.)

> Translated from the Swedish ms. by Jacques de Coussanges.

—— Les Fravashis: Étude sur les traces dans le mazdéisme d'une ancienne conception sur la survivance des morts. Paris, 1899.

Spiegel, Fr. Erânische Alterthumskunde. Vol. 2, Leipzig, 1873. Pages 158–167.

Stave, Erik. Über den Einfluss des Parsismus auf das Judentum. Haarlem, 1898. Pages 145–204.

Tiele, C. P. Geschichte der Religion im Altertum bis auf Alexander den Grossen. (Deutsche autorisierte Ausgabe von G. Gehrich.) 2 vols., Gotha, 1896, 1903. Vol. 2: Die Religion bei den iranischen Völkern.

> See esp. pages 297–310, 'Das Leben nach dem Tode und die Eschatologie.'

—— The Religion of the Iranian Peoples. Translated from the German by G. K. Nariman. Part 1, Bombay, 1912.'

A translation of the first three chapters of the preceding work.

Wesendonk, O. G. von. Urmensch und Seele in der iranischen Überlieferung. Hannover, 1924. Pages 191–202: 'Das Schicksal der Seele.'

West, E. W. Notes on Zarathuśtra's Doctrine regarding the Soul. In *JRAS.* 1899, p. 605–611.

Windischmann, Fr. Zoroastrische Studien. Berlin, 1863. Pages 231–259.

THE ZOROASTRIAN DOCTRINE OF A FUTURE LIFE

FROM DEATH TO THE INDIVIDUAL JUDGMENT

CHAPTER I
INTRODUCTION

Yōi mōi ahmāi sǝraošǝm dąn čayascā
upā.jimǝn haurvātā amǝrǝtātā vaŋhǝ̄uš
mainyǝ̄uš šyaoθanāiš.
— Gāthā Ushtavaitī, Ys. 45. 5.

Zarathushtra's message of immortality. 'All those who will give hearing for Me unto this one (the Prophet) will come unto Salvation and Immortality through the works of the Good Spirit'—such was the promise given by Ahura Mazdāh to those who accepted the Religion of Zarathushtra, the Prophet of Ancient Iran, and such were the words in which the Supreme Deity vouchsafed the revelation to him. Divinely inspired and strongly convinced of his own mission, the Prophet (*mąθran*) delivered his message (*dūtya*) to mankind nearly three thousand years ago. It was a message full of hope for the future. It throbbed with a pious expectation of a world perfected in the present life and to be realized in all its fulness in the world beyond. We can understand the echo which it found in the heart of the folk when he appeared as the spiritual leader (*ratav*) of Old Iran in the bygone ages of history. Nor has its ringing truth been forgotten today.

Zarathushtra's pre-eminent concern with the bearing of eschatology on conduct can easily be seen from a study of the Gāthās. Faith and works form the foundation of the doctrine of salvation in the religion of Ancient Iran. A belief in the freedom of the will, in the acknowledgment of man's ability to choose the right or to choose the wrong, and in his consequent responsibility to his Creator, lies at the basis of the moral and ethical system of the Zoroastrian religion, which above all emphasizes the existence of the two warring principles of Good and Evil, Light and Darkness. To guide man to the choice of right, and thus to assure his gaining eternal salvation, was the very purpose of Zarathushtra's mission upon earth.

The very words 'Salvation' (*haurvatāt*), or the essence of wholesome completeness in a spiritual sense—that personified 'saving health' with all the connotation of the term as used in Christianity—and 'Immortality' (*amərətāt*) in the life eternal have already struck this note. Not this world alone, which the Prophet sought to improve through his teachings, but the outlook for a world regenerate, made perfect and renewed (*fərašōm kərənāun ahūm, fəračōtəma*, etc.), formed the burden of his Gāthās, 'Hymns' or 'Psalms.' He visualized all this as the sovereign rule, dominion, and power, 'the Kingdom' (*xšaθra*) to come, when mankind, regenerate and individually judged, should bring to pass the final Renovation (*frašōkərəti*) of the world. As a 'Savior,' or, perhaps more literally, as 'He who will be the Benefactor' (*saošyant*), Zarathushtra came forward with his message of endless hope and cheerful optimism, which has never failed to animate the hearts of his followers. It may be that in later times the religion which he founded looked forward to the fulfilment of his prophetic view through the appearance in successive millenniums of three Saoshyants spiritually born of his seed, and in many other points gave more concrete form to his ideal conceptions; but, as we study the sources, from his own words preserved in the Gāthās, the *ipsissima verba* of the Prophet, down through the centuries, we shall always find the belief in the future life and the heavenly world present as one of the main currents in Zoroastrian thought.

The sources in general. The sacred writings of the Zoroastrian Faith, from the earliest texts to the latest works that deal with the Religion, bear abundant witness to what has been stated above, as will be shown in the course of the following investigation. The examination is naturally based upon the texts comprised in the Avestan canon itself, and upon the traditional literature in Pahlavi as developed in Sasanian times and afterwards, supplemented later by the religious writings in Parsi-Persian.

It were to be wished that we had some material to add from the Old Persian inscriptions of the Achaemenian Kings, since these monuments in stone present records which are most nearly akin to the Avesta in religion and language.[1] We do not find in them, however, any mention of a future life; the blessings which are prayed for and the imprecations which are invoked are purely of a temporal character.[2] The absence of specific reference to the life hereafter may be due perhaps to the official character of these records ($ha^ndugā$) and to their limited extent.

The silence of these official records would not be so significant if we felt assured that we could accept as corroborative testimony certain references made by Greek writers to the religious beliefs of the Achaemenian rulers,[3] but these do not concern this particular part of our study and are reserved for treatment later.

It is clear in any case, however, that the later Greek authors were acquainted with the doctrine of the Frashōkereti,[4] but since again these references relate rather to eschatology proper

[1] See Clemen, *Nachrichten pers. Religion*, p. 54–94; cf. further Jackson in *GIrPh.* 2. 687–693, and also Gray in *ERE.* 1. 69–73.

[2] For example, the Behistan inscription of Darius, col. 4. 54–59: 'may Auramazdā be thy friend ($dauštā$) and thy family be numerous, and mayest thou live long ($dargam\ jīvā$) . . . (But, if wicked,) may Auramazdā be thy smiter ($ja^ntā$) and there be no family to thee.' Cf. also Bh. col. 4. 73–80.

[3] Cf., for example, the words of Prexaspes as recorded by Herodotus (3.62), see Clemen, *op. cit.* p. 123; or again the speech placed on the lips of the dying Cyrus the Great by Xenophon in the *Cyropaedia* (8. 7. 17–24), see Clemen, *op. cit.* p. 89.

[4] Among such references would be Theopompus (flourished B.C. 338) as quoted by Diogenes Laertius (flourished c. A.D. 210), *Prooem.* 6, 9; Plutarch (c. A.D. 46–120), *Isis and Osiris*, ch. 47; Aeneas of Gaza (flourished at the beginning of the sixth century), *Theophrastus*, 77; also others. Cf. Jackson in *GIrPh.* 2. 684; Clemen, *op. cit.* p. 123, 128–131, 167–169, 215; also Moulton, *EZ.* p. 415–417.

than to the immediate fate of the soul, they may simply be mentioned here, but reserved for presentation elsewhere. Laying aside such classical evidences, we may now turn to the direct Zoroastrian sources themselves, beginning with the Gāthās.

The Gāthās. The Gāthās, as being the oldest part of the Avesta and embodying the veritable words of Zarathushtra (seventh century B.C. or earlier),[5] naturally form the starting-point from which to proceed in our research. These Gāthās, 'hymns, psalms,' are akin to the verses of the Vedic bards. They contain the teachings of the Prophet, summed up in metrical stanzas which he composed as a nucleus of his discourses.[6] These anthems of divine praise are always spoken of as 'the Holy Gāthās' (gāθā́ ašaonīš) from an early date (cf. for example, Ys. 55. 1). Their language is more archaic and somewhat different from that used elsewhere in the Avesta. The style of expression is exceedingly lofty, and the ideas are prevailingly abstract in character, so that the interpretation of some of the passages affords great difficulty.

The Gāthās,[7] comprising seventeen hymns in all, are arranged

[5] For views regarding the much-discussed question of the date of Zarathushtra see Jackson, *Zoroaster, the Prophet of Ancient Iran*, p. 150–178 (New York, 1899), who makes a strong case in favor of accepting the date that stands in the Parsi tradition, namely B.C. 660–583. So also Meillet, *Trois conférences sur les Gāthā* (Paris, 1925), p. 21–32. Hertel, in a recent monograph, *Die Zeit Zoroasters* (Leipzig, 1924), advances arguments in support of a still later date, according to which (p. 47) Zarathushtra must have been alive in 522 B.C. and probably after that date also. Charpentier, in *BSOS*. (London, 1925), 3. 747–755, refutes this 'new theory' and is in favor of a much earlier date, namely (p. 754) 'somewhere in the neighborhood of 1000–900 B.C.—or perhaps even somewhat earlier.' This he holds 'with Eduard Meyer, Andreas, Clemen, Bartholomae, and others.' See especially Bartholomae, *Zarathuštra's Leben und Lehre*, p. 10–11 (Heidelberg, 1924), and compare Geldner in *Encyclopaedia Britannica*, 11th ed., 21. 246, but particularly 28. 1041.

[6] The theory that the Gāthās presuppose a frame-work of prose no longer extant is mentioned by Jackson, *Av. Grammar*, introd. p. 18; see also Geldner in *GIrPh*. 2. 29; Bartholomae, *Die Gatha's des Awesta*, introd. p. 4–5; and cf. especially Meillet, *Trois Conférences sur les Gāthā*, p. 39–52.

[7] For a detailed description of the contents, arrangement, extent, and character of the Gāthās and the Later Avesta, see Geldner, 'Awestalitteratur,' in *GIrPh*. 2. 1–53.

in five groups, the Gāthā Ahunavaitī (Ys. 28–34), Ushtavaitī (Ys. 43–46), Spentā Mainyū (Ys. 47–50), Vohukhshathrā (Ys. 51), and Vahishtōishti (Ys. 53). This grouping as a pentad is based on the scheme of the meters employed; we have no knowledge, however, of what the original order of the seventeen may have been. In any case, their importance is recognized by their position as the very center of the whole Yasna.

Between the first two of these Gāthic groups is interpolated the so-called Yasna Haptanghāiti, or 'Yasna of the Seven Chapters' (Ys. 35–42). Its language is as archaic as that of the Gāthās, but the form of composition is almost entirely prose. In age these 'Seven Chapters' would rank next after the Gāthās, but their special contents yield little if anything for the purpose of our present investigation.

The Later Avesta. Though the Gāthās are preponderantly eschatological in character, they deal much more with principles than with details. The later Avestan texts, sometimes termed the Younger Avesta, consequently serve to develop the picture outlined in those older documents. The Later Avesta, or remaining portion of the sacred canon so far as extant,[8] may be classified, according to the commonly adopted arrangement, into the following divisions, or books. First in order comes the Yasna, 'sacrifice, worship,' the chief liturgical work of the sacred canon. It consists principally of ascriptions of praise and prayer, and, together with the Gāthās and the Yasna Haptanghāiti, it comprises seventy-two chapters. Then comes the Visprat (or Vīspered, as it is sometimes called), the book of invocations and offerings to 'all the lords' (Av. *vīspe ratavō*). It consists of additions to portions of the Yasna, which it resembles in language and in form, and comprises twenty-four chapters. Third in order come the Yashts (Av. *yešti*, 'worship by laudation'), consisting of twenty-one hymns in praise of various divinities or 'worshipful ones' (Av. *yazata*). Together

[8] See above, page 4, note 7.

with these Yashts may be grouped certain minor texts, consisting of brief prayers and constituting what is called the Khvartak Apastāk (or Khorda Avesta). The last book of the sacred canon is the Vidēvdāt (or the Vendīdād, as it is commonly known), 'law against the demons,' a priestly code in twenty-two chapters. Besides the above texts there are a number of fragments, which are pieces surviving from the other Nasks, or divisions of the Avesta, no longer extant. The most important of these fragments, in the present connection, are those from the Hadhōkht Nask, and what is generally known as the Vishtāsp Yasht. Of minor importance are the Avestan quotations contained in the Nīrangastān, the Aogemadaēchā, and the Vicharkart i Dēnīk.

Although the books of the Later Avesta differ greatly in theme and style, they may be regarded in general as contemporaneous with the Achaemenian rule (B.C. 558–323) in Persia, although some portions may belong to the succeeding centuries.

The Pahlavi literature. The subject of our study is developed further in the Pahlavi books, which belong mainly to the Sasanian period (A.D. 226–651), when Zoroastrianism enjoyed both material prosperity and a spiritual revival.

The Pahlavi literature [9] may here be conveniently divided into two classes. First, Pahlavi translations (or versions) of the Avestan texts, intermingled with Pahlavi commentary. The work of translating the scriptures into the current idiom may already have begun during the latter part of the Parthian period. (B.C. 250–A.D. 226), and must have been completed at the latest during the reign of Shahpuhar II (A.D. 309–380), when the final revision of the Avestan texts was made by Āturpāt i Mahraspandān. Second, independent Pahlavi treatises on matters connected with religion. The importance of these latter Pahlavi texts can hardly be overestimated. They often preserve old material no longer extant in its Avestan form,

[9] For a detailed description of the extent and character of the Pahlavi literature and the later Parsi-Persian writings, see West, 'Pahlavi Literature,' in *GIrPh.* 2. 75–129.

and thus supplement the lacunae in the earlier doctrinal scheme, besides elaborating and adding to the data already found in the Avesta. It may be noted further that some of these Pahlavi works were either completed, though begun earlier, or written in their entirety during the rule of the Abbasids (A.D. 749-847), after the downfall of the Sasanian Empire. Additions seem to have been made to some Pahlavi works as late as the end of the eleventh century.

Among these independent Pahlavi treatises the most important for our investigation are (1) the Bundahishn,[10] 'creation of the beginning,' or 'original creation,' a sort of Iranian Genesis and Revelation, based upon the old Dāmdāt Nask of the Avesta; (2) the Dēnkart, 'acts of the religion,' an encyclopaedia of Zoroastrianism; (3) the Artāk Vīrāz Nāmak, 'book of Saint Vīrāz,' or a Dantesque vision of Heaven and Hell; (4) the Dātastān i Dēnīk, 'religious ordinances or opinions,' together with (5) the Pahlavi Rivāyat accompanying this theological treatise; (6) the Dātastān i Mēnūk i Khrat, 'ordinances of the Spirit of Wisdom'; (7) the Shāyist nē-Shāyist, 'the proper and the improper'; and (8) the Shkand-vimānīk Vichār, 'doubt-dispelling expositions.' Of minor importance for our purpose, and seldom cited, are (9) the Handarz i Āturpāt i Mahraspandān, 'admonitions of Āturpāt, son of Mahraspand'; (10) the Handarz i Hōsrav i Kavātān, 'admonitions of Hōsrav, son of Kavāt'; (11) the Ganj i Shāhīkān, 'treasure of the royal depository,' a book of good counsel, containing gems of wisdom; and finally (12) the Vichītakīhā i Zātsparam, 'selections of Zātsparam.'

The Parsi-Persian writings. In surveying the literary material we must include the priestly writings of later times (dating after the eleventh century), the so-called Modern-Persian Zoroastrian literature of the Parsis.[11] The principal and doubtless

[10] There exist two recensions of the Bundahishn, one Indian and the other Iranian; see below, page 12, note 16.

[11] See above, page 6, note 9.

earliest book among these is the prose Sad Dar, a treatise on
'a hundred subjects' connected with the Parsi religion. There
exist two metrical versions of the Sad Dar, known as 'the short-
meter version' (composed in 1496) and 'the long-meter version'
(composed in 1605). The exact date of the writing of the prose
Sad Dar has not yet been ascertained, but we can safely conjecture that it was already a very old book when the metrical
versions were composed.[12] The second in order is the Sad
Dar Bundahish, or the 'Bundahish of a hundred chapters'
(composed some time before 1528), detailing in a hundred sections the chief customs and religious laws of the Parsis.[13] Both
these treatises are very often quoted in the later Persian Rivāyats, or collections of religious traditions (compiled between
the years 1478 and 1773 A.D.).[14] The most important of these
latter writings, which stand third in order both as regards age
and as regards contents, is the Rivāyat of Dārāb Hormazdyār. It may be noted that it is the most complete and
systematically arranged among the so-called classified Rivāyats.
It was compiled in A.D. 1679, and a Gujarati version of it was
made by the author at a later date.

Present-day ceremonies. Further light may be thrown on
the whole subject by the discussions added here and there to
bring out the significance of certain of Zarathushtra's tenets
which are observed today by the Parsis in their ceremonies
connected with the dead, and which give assurance of life eternal
in Paradise to the faithful who follow the religion of Zarathushtra,
the Prophet of Ancient Iran.

[12] For additional details as to this book, see below, page 18.
[13] For further remarks, see below, page 18.
[14] See also below, page 19, note 48.

CHAPTER II

THE SOUL OF THE RIGHTEOUS DURING THE FIRST THREE NIGHTS AFTER DEATH

Introduction. As to the fate of the soul [1] immediately after death,[2] the Gāthās do not provide us with a clear picture. The Later Avesta, however, contains several passages explicitly describing how the soul of the righteous or of the wicked is believed to hover near its earthly tenement, in confidence or in fear, for three days and three nights before it passes to the individual judgment. The Pahlavi and the Parsi-Persian texts not only paraphrase the Avestan material with elaboration of detail but also contribute some new ideas concerning the state of the soul during this period of suspense.

I

The soul of the righteous in the Later Avesta. According to the description in the Hadhōkht Nask, when a righteous

[1] The Avestan word for 'soul' is *urvan* (= Phl. *ruvān*, NP. *ravān*), and constitutes one of the most important psychological concepts in Zoroastrianism. The etymology has been much disputed and seems obscure (see Casartelli, 'Avestan *Urvan*, "Soul,"' in *A Volume of Oriental Studies presented to E. G. Browne*, p. 127-128, Cambridge, 1922). The etymology (*var*-, 'choose') suggested by Jackson (in *GIrPh*. 2. 674) seems to suit the sense perfectly, because *urvan* is the spiritual faculty which exercises free will, the power of choosing between good and evil. As to the five spiritual faculties of man, recognized in the Avesta, see below, p. 33, n. 1; and cf. especially Jackson, *GIrPh*. 2. 674-675, and now Wesendonk, *Urmensch und Seele*, p. 191-202.

[2] According to Zoroastrianism, death means the cessation of physical life, caused by the separation of the soul from the body; cf. Vd. 5. 37; 7. 1, 2; 8. 81; 9. 43; 13. 12. According to the Iranian Bundahishn the five constituents of human personality (independent of the fivefold division of the spiritual faculties of man, noted above), which are *tan* (body), *jān* (life, vitality), *ruvān* (soul), *ēvīnak* (form), and *frōhar* (Fravashi), are separated at death; the body returns to the earth, the life to the wind, the form to the sun, and the soul is joined to the Fravashi, so that the soul cannot be destroyed. (See the text of IrBd. given by Darmesteter, *ZA*. 2. 500.) Cf. also Jackson, *GIrPh*. 2. 674, and Moulton, *EZ*. p. 163, 256 n. 2.

9

man passes away, his soul takes its seat near the head,³ chanting the sacred hymns and proclaiming the happiness which Ahura Mazdāh will accord to the blest:—

Zarathushtra asked Ahura Mazdāh: 'O Ahura Mazdāh, most holy Spirit, Creator of the material world, Thou Holy One! When a righteous one dies, where does his soul abide that night?'

Ahura Mazdāh answered: 'It takes its seat near the head, chanting the Ushtavaitī Gāthā,⁴ proclaiming happiness: "Salvation is his to whomsoever Ahura Mazdāh, ruling at will, shall give salvation!"⁵ On that night his soul experiences as much joy as all that which (he experienced as) a living being.'⁶

'Where does his soul abide on the second night?'

Ahura Mazdāh answered: 'It takes its seat near the head, chanting the Ushtavaitī Gāthā, proclaiming happiness: "Salvation is his to whomsoever Ahura Mazdāh, ruling at will, shall give salvation!" On that

---

³ According to the Parsi mode of disposing of the dead, the body of the deceased, washed and clothed in white, is laid on slabs of stone in a corner of the anteroom of his house where a part of the funeral ceremony is performed. The corpse is so placed as to avoid having the head point towards the north.

⁴ The name of the second Gāthā (Ys. 43-46). The quotation here refers, not to the Gāthā as a whole, but only to its first section, viz. Ys. 43, which begins with the word *uštā*. The selection of the sacred psalm as the Song of Joy, though arbitrary, is yet well made. See also the summary of the Phl. comm. on the chapter, as contained in the Sūtkar, Varshtmānsar, and Bagha Nasks, as summarized in Dk. 9. 13, 36, 58 (cf. *SBE*. 37. 195, 269, 353).

⁵ Such is evidently the way in which the writer of the Nask interpreted the abridged quotation from Ys. 43. 1, where the first *uštā* is really an adv., while here it is understood as a subst. (nom. sg.), as in phrases like *ušta tē*, cf. Vd. 7. 52; Ys. 9. 25; Yt. 17. 7; see Bthl. *AirWb*. 417. The catechetical commentary on the verse quoted, as contained in Ys. 21. 3, 4, is of considerable interest, as placing the promise of salvation on the lips of Ahura.

⁶ The words *juyō aṇhuš* are here taken as referring to him as a living being in general. Somewhat differently Darmesteter, *SBE*. 23. 314 (= *ZA*. 2. 651) and Bthl. *AirWb*. 610. The sense conveyed by the last line is well brought out by the Phl. version, viz. that the soul enjoys as much pleasure during that night as it had felt during its whole life on earth.

night his soul experiences as much joy as all that which (he experienced as) a living being.'

'Where does his soul abide on the third night?'

Ahura Mazdāh answered: 'It takes its seat near the head, chanting the Ushtavaitī Gāthā, proclaiming happiness: "Salvation is his to whomsoever Ahura Mazdāh, ruling at will, shall give salvation!" And that night his soul experiences as much joy as all that which (he experienced as) a living being.' [7]

Thus during the first, second, and third nights after death the soul of the pious sings in exaltation the Song of Salvation, beginning with the verse: *uštā ahmāi yahmāi uštā kahmāicit*.

The Vishtāsp Yasht gives a similar description of the immediate experience that attends the soul of the righteous, and it further adds (VYt. 54 = Yt. 24. 54) that 'during the first night his soul abides (*vaṇhaiti*) in [the state of] good word (*hūxte*), during the second night in [that of the] good deed (*hvaršte*), and during the third night at the dividing of the ways (*paθąm paiti vī-čarənā̊*).' [8] Of these two paths, one leads to felicity, the other to perdition.[9] Therefore these are the ways which are open, 'one to the wicked, and one to the righteous,' i.e. the Chinvat Bridge, as mentioned in the Vidēvdāt.[10]

The Avestan texts do not state explicitly what other experiences befall the soul of the pious during these three nights, but

[7] HN. 2 (= Yt. 22). 1–6.

[8] The Westergaard text (p. 310–311) has *paθā̊* . . . *čičarənā̊*, which should probably be emended to *paθąm* . . . *vī-čarənā̊*, as in Ys. 42. 1, Yt. 11. 4; so also Bthl. *AirWb*. 847, 1437. The interpretation of the last words in this sentence, as here given, seems more appropriate both from the standpoint of grammar and of sense than that of Darmesteter in *SBE*. 23. 343 (= *ZA*. 2. 681). Cf. Vd. 19. 29; see below, pages 63–64.

[9] VYt. (= Yt. 24). 54. It is to be noted that VYt. 53–64 are borrowed, though slightly altered, from the first part of HN. 2 (i.e. § 1–18), which describes the fate of the righteous. The last section (§ 65) of VYt. quotes the Kimā Gāthā (cf. HN. 2. 20), showing that the second part of HN. 2 (i.e. § 19–36), describing the fate of the wicked, should have followed there.

[10] Vd. 19. 29; cf. page 64, below.

we may infer from the developments in the Pahlavi literature [11] that the demon Vīzaresha, who awaits the soul at the Chinvat Bridge,[12] makes a fruitless attack on it beforehand and struggles in vain to capture it. In the attempt the other 'wicked malicious demons' may be thought to join, namely, those who 'cut the thread' of life,[13] and especially Astō-vīdhātu and the evil Vayu, who would naturally seek to kill the soul as they do the body.[14] Probably for that reason the angel Sraosha is invoked in the Avesta to protect in both lives 'against the onslaughts of Aēshma, which the evil-minded Aēshma, together with the demon-created Vīdhātu, launches.'[15]

II

The soul of the righteous in Pahlavi literature. The Avestan doctrine, as set forth in the significant passages cited above, is stated in even more fully developed form in the Pahlavi books.

The Iranian Bundahishn,[16] to begin with, furnishes us with a vivid picture of the immediate fate of the soul of the righteous and of the wicked alike, and the passage is worth translating literally.

> When men die, the soul sits for three nights near the place where his head was; and on those nights, (he) who (is) the demon Vīzarsh, with (his) associates (*hamkārān*), looks at them (i.e. the souls) with great intent (*vas handāč*),[17] and always turning his back to

---

[11] See below, pages 12–13, 15–16.
[12] Vd. 19. 29.
[13] Vd. 19. 28. For the interpretation of this phrase, see below, p. 62, n. 12.
[14] Vd. 5. 8, 9.
[15] Ys. 57. 25; cf. similarly (but applied to Mithra) Yt. 10. 93. For references in Pahlavi literature, see below, pages 83–85.
[16] On the general characteristics of the Indian and Iranian recensions of the Bundahishn (here designated as Bd. and IrBd. respectively), see West, *Pahlavi Literature*, in *GIrPh*. 2. 98–102; Anklesaria, *Būndahishn*, introd. p. xix–xxxvi.
[17] Better so, than to read *ān šap* with Modi; cf. Modi, *An Untranslated Chapter of the Bundehesh*, p. 58, n. 27 (full title is given below in n. 21).

DURING THE FIRST THREE NIGHTS AFTER DEATH 13

the fire [18] which is kindled there. Therefore fire is kept burning during those three nights till day, at the place where his head was. When the fire is not (kindled there), he (i.e. Vīzarsh) keeps his back turned to the Ātash-varahrām (Fire) or (*aδāv*) to the Fires which are of like grandeur (*hamawrank*).

During [19] the three nights, when cutting (*karīnišn*) and dissolution (*višōpišn*) [20] come upon the body, then there seems to him to be as much distress as there does to a man when his house is destroyed. During those three days the soul sits near the head (lit. the top part of the body) with the hope that 'it may so happen that the blood may be warmed up (*xōn tapēt*) and the breath may enter the body (*vāt ō tan ravēt*), so that I may be able to go once more [into the body].' [21]

The Pahlavi text then goes on to depict the happy experiences of the soul of the righteous alone:—

And after the third night, at dawn,[22] if the soul be pious, it says thus: 'Happy [23] is he by whom that which is his (becomes) the happiness of anyone else

---

[18] See below, page 16, note 36.

[19] A new paragraph should begin here and run on to the next. Differently Dr. Modi.

[20] Modi, 'pain and misery.'

[21] IrBd. 30. 2, 3 (= Modi, *An Untranslated Chapter of the Bundehesh*, in *JBBRAS.* 21. 49–65; reprinted in his *Asiatic Papers*, I. 217–234, Bombay, 1905). The chapter is the 30th in order in Anklesaria's edition (see his introd. p. xxvi, col. B). Better so numbered than 37th, as taken by West in *SBE.* 5, introd. p. 37, and accepted by Modi. The Pahlavi text of this chapter is found in Anklesaria's *Būndahishn* (photo-zincograph facsimile), p. 199–205.

[22] Instead of 'during the first three nights,' as in other accounts regarding the fate of the soul.

[23] The Av. word *uštā* is translated in the Pahlavi by *nēwak* (*nēk*), which means 'good, beautiful, happy, blessed.' This is a translation of the opening of the Ushtavaitī Gāthā; cf. page 10, above.

< that is, (if) I am good, everybody will be good through me >. Ōharmazd, through His sovereign will, granted (happiness) to me.'[24]

The Artāk Vīrāz Nāmak in its turn describes the vision seen by Vīrāz. During the first night of his journey from the realms of the living to those of the dead, having been welcomed by the angels Srōsh (Religious Obedience) and Ātar (Fire) as guides, he saw from the vantage point of the Chinvat Bridge the soul of a pious man who had just departed this life, hovering near the head of his corpse and chanting the words of the Gāthā stanza noted above.[25] On the whole, the account given in this work is nearly the same as that found in the Hadhōkht Nask of the Avesta and need not be repeated here.

The Pahlavi Rivāyat accompanying the Dātastān i Dēnīk[26] likewise closely follows the Hadhōkht Nask, but adds one detail to the composite picture, which may be worth noting here. It tells us that the soul of the righteous, as it rests near its earthly tenement during the three days, appears clothed in white raiment (*vastrak i spēt dārēt*).

The Dātastān i Dēnīk offers much new material on the subject. According to this text, when a righteous man passes away, his soul remains on earth for three nights, doubtful about its allotted destination (*gās*) and in fear of the Accounting (*hamār*) at the Judgment Seat. As it sits there beholding its own good and wicked deeds,[27] it experiences trepidation concerning the crossing of the Chinvat Bridge, yet feels assured of the good outcome because —

[24] IrBd. 30. 3.
[25] AVN. 4. 1–14. The account of the journey commences with this chapter.
[26] PhlRiv. 23. 1–4 (= PhlHN. 2. 1–6), ed. Dhabhar, p. 81–82. The Pahlavi treatise deals with a great variety of miscellaneous texts on Parsi ceremonies, customs, traditions, and contains much legendary material. It devotes a full chapter to the fate of the soul, § 1–17 dealing with that of the righteous, and § 18–35 dealing with that of the wicked. The account closely follows the Pahlavi version of HN. 2.
[27] DD. 24. 1, 2.

DURING THE FIRST THREE NIGHTS AFTER DEATH

the soul obtains, during the first night, pleasure (*rāmišn*) from its own good thoughts; the second night from its own good words; and the third night from its own good deeds. And if, along with its righteousness, there be any sin, even though it may be (merely) in its beginning (*pa būn ēstēt*), the first retribution (*pātfrās*) [28] in atonement (*tōčišn*) for the wicked deeds occurs during the same third night.[29]

Thus the soul of the pious, if it is not absolutely righteous, has to undergo some part of the punishment accorded to the wicked for his sins of commission and omission.

The same book describes how 'happiness' comes to the soul on the first night on account of its good thoughts, but 'annoyance' (*bēš*) because of its former evil thoughts; it experiences 'pleasure' on the second night on account of its good words, but 'discomfort' (*dušxᵛārīh*) because of its former evil words; and, on the third night, it enjoys 'exaltation' on account of its good deeds, yet some 'retribution' (*pātfrās*) is visited upon the soul owing to its evil deeds.[30]

It is during these three nights, according to the Bundahishn, that the demon Vīzarsh, noted above, struggles with the souls of men that have passed away.[31] With his devilish crew he tries to ensnare the soul of the righteous, casting a noose (*band*) around its neck to drag it off to hell; but he fails in his attempt and the snare falls off.[32]

Contrary to the spirit of the Avesta, the Pahlavi writers picture the newly departed soul as more or less helpless, and they indulge in elaborate descriptions of how it must rely upon

[28] The second retribution occurs at the Chinvat Bridge (see DD. 24. 6); see below, page 78.

[29] DD. 24. 4. This is one of the instances in which the author displays practical wisdom and originality of thought; he seems to assume that the righteous soul is not without some faults which must be expiated.

[30] DD. 20. 1, 2; cf. also West in *SBE*. 18. 46.

[31] Bd. 28. 18; IrBd. 30. 2; see above, pages 12–13.

[32] PhlVd. 19. 29, comm.; cf. below, page 63, note 22.

the righteous Srōsh for protection from evil influences. Srōsh will afford this guardianship if he is properly propitiated by the surviving relatives [33]; and hence among the Zoroastrians from Sasanian times onwards great importance has been attached to the ceremonies [34] performed in his honor during the period while the soul is presumed still to remain in this world. Its state at this critical moment is frequently compared in the Pahlavi texts to that of a new-born infant, which requires care and protection from the demons,[35] and for this reason a bright fire should be kept constantly burning during these three days near the place where the body of the deceased was laid.[36]

A significant question is asked in the Pahlavi texts as to whether the soul (*ruvān*) is conscious of suffering while the body (*tan*) is resolved into its elements (*banjišn*) [37] at death. The Dātastān i Dēnīk states that when once the soul has departed from the body, the corpse itself is inert, unmoving and devoid of feeling; but the soul, through its spiritual perception, is aware of what is taking place,[38] though this causes no distress in the case of a soul destined for salvation. We are expressly told, furthermore, that the soul of the righteous, while seeing the body thus destroyed, is filled with great joy, being confident of attaining to the Best Existence which is really in sight as a result of the merits it has accumulated while in the body. Such

---

[33] Bd. 30. 29; ŠNŠ. 17. 3; DD. 28. 6; see below, p. 18–19, 25–26.

[34] The locus classicus for these ceremonies is PhlVd. 8. 22, comm.; also ŠNŠ. 17. 3–5 and DD. 81. 12–15. A reference to such ceremonies may perhaps be found in a passage of the early Christian writer Arnobius (about 300 A.D.), *Adversus Nationes*, 2. 62: 'The Magians assert that they have commendatory prayers by which some powers or other are appeased and make the road easy for those who are striving to fly up to heaven.' Cf. Clemen, *Pers. Religion*, p. 191–192; also Böklen, *Pars. Eschatologie*, p. 38. See p. 86, n. 76.

[35] DD. 28. 2–6; 81. 3.

[36] IrBd. 30. 2; DD. 28. 4, 5. This custom is observed among the Parsis to this day, the fire being kept constantly burning for three days, as also near the cradle of a new-born babe. (Cf. also ŠNŠ. 12. 11–12, and SD. 16. 1–3.)

[37] See above, page 9, note 2; and later, page 33, note 1.

[38] DD. 16. 1–3; cf. also PhlRiv. 24. 1 (ed. Dhabhar, p. 89).

a soul is equally certain of the Final Renovation, when life shall once more be united with the flesh, and consequently it utters a cry spiritually that, even if the organized body (*tan i pasāxt*) is thus destroyed at death,

> at last the body (*tan*) and life (*jān*) shall be joined [39] at the time of the Resurrection.[40]

This thought of the Resurrection becomes a source of happiness and hope to the spirit of the body and also to other good spirits, but is fear and torment to the demons and fiends.[41]

A somewhat different point of view is presented both in the passage from the Iranian Bundahishn, already cited, and in the Dēnkart (9. 16. 6). The latter passage is particularly important on account of its presumably being taken out of the old Sūtkar Nask. According to this text the consciousness (*bōδ*) remains near the body (*tan*), and tries to protect the corpse from the coming dissolution (*višōpišn*). As it sees the body being destroyed, it feels great unhappiness (*ašātīh*), and its grief and alarm are compared to the panic felt by a ewe when she sees one of her young in danger and rushes to its rescue. The distress felt by the consciousness increases as it reflects on the misery (*hanākīh*) and dissolution that has come upon the once happy and beautiful body.[42]

[39] According to the teaching of the Avesta, the form (*kəhrp*) or body (*tanu*) is once more renewed at the Resurrection (see Yt. 13. 61; WFr. 4. 3, cf. Haas, 'An Avestan Fragment on the Resurrection,' in *Spiegel Memorial Volume*, p. 181–187, Bombay, 1908). The individual assumes the new body of the hereafter (Phl. *tan i pasīn*) at the rejuvenescence or renewal of the world (*frašōkərəti*). See Jackson, *GIrPh.* 2. 674. Further discussion of this subject is reserved for my monograph, to be published later, on the Zoroastrian Doctrine of a General Judgment.

[40] DD. 16. 7. West (in *SBE.* 18. 38) translates this somewhat differently.

[41] DD. 16. 8.

[42] Dk. 9. 16. 6–7; cf. West, *SBE.* 37. 201, and Sanjana, vol. 17, text, p. 36–37, tr. p. 29–30.

III

The soul of the righteous in Parsi-Persian literature.
By way of supplement we may briefly mention the account of the subject contained in the Parsi-Persian literature of the post-Sasanian period. Among these works the most important and the most often quoted by the Parsi compilers of the Persian Rivāyats, or religious 'traditions,' are the treatises known as Sad Dar,[43] properly so called, and the Sad Dar Bundahish.[44]

The Sad Dar Bundahish, alone among these late Zoroastrian writings, contains a detailed description of the immediate fate of the souls of the righteous and the wicked, undoubtedly following the Pahlavi accounts. The soul's experience during the first days after death is described as follows:—

> It is said in the Revelation (*dēn*), that when life (*jān*) goes out of the body (*tan*), the soul (*ravān*) remains in this world for three days. It goes to the place where it departed from the body, and longs for the body, and wishes that it may once more be within the body.[45]

Both the Sad Dar and the Sad Dar Bundahish speak at length about the advantages of a person's celebrating a ceremony for his 'living soul' (*zinda ravān*),[46] and thus propitiating the angel Srōsh in advance, so that when the man passes away, Srōsh may keep watch over his soul during the first three days and nights and protect it from harm at the hands of Ahriman and the demons. The chief advantage of this anticipatory act

[43] There are two metrical versions of the Sad Dar now extant besides the prose original. See Dhabhar, introd. p. 5.

[44] These treatises and works of a like nature are sometimes called 'Old Rivāyats' as distinguished from the so-called 'New or Greater Rivāyats.'

[45] SDBd. 99. 1. The chapter is translated here (see also p. 44) for the first time. For the text see ed. Dhabhar, p. 168–170. It is of interest to note that the whole chapter is quoted in the RivDH., vol. 1, p. 149–151, though the compiler fails to draw attention to the fact.

[46] This has become the technical term for the ceremony among the Parsis. For the description of the rite see Modi, *Religious Ceremonies*, p. 444–446.

of piety is that, if his death occurs in a place where there is no one to perform the usual three-night ceremonies in honor of Srōsh, the celebrant's soul has already received the necessary protection and desired salvation; and since a rite for the living soul has been celebrated, there are no arrears for him, and he is free.[47]

The Parsi-Persian Rivāyats,[48] with their usual emphasis on the performance of rituals, lay special stress on the ceremonies in honor of Srōsh. They depict the soul as being harassed on all sides by Ahriman and his demonic host; it is compared to a sheep pursued by a wolf, or to a traveler who has lost his way; protection is afforded by Srōsh alone, and the ceremonies in his honor are therefore indispensable. We give here *in extenso* the passage from the Rivāyat of Kāmā Bahrā, which is not available to scholars in translation.

> And it is said in the Revelation thus: 'When life is separated from the body, the wicked Ahriman, together with all the demons, tries to capture the soul in order that they may drag it to hell. The soul is frightened by Ahriman and his demonic host, just as a sheep is frightened by a wolf. It is pursued by demons, as one chased by a powerful enemy. The soul is harassed and perplexed in the same manner as a traveler who has lost his way. During those three days when the soul remains on earth, it suffers greater distress and misery than is experienced by the wicked in hell for a period of nine thousand years.[49]

---

[47] SD. 58. 1–12. Cf. also SD. 47. 3; 87. 1; SDBd. 43 (= ed. Dhabhar p. 113–114); RivDH. vol. 2, p. 35–42 (cf. Gujarati vers. p. 87–88).

[48] These Rivāyats, properly so-called, were compiled mostly during the fifteenth, sixteenth, seventeenth, and eighteenth centuries A.D. (1478–1773), and as such they are too modern to be accepted as authorities in matters religious.

[49] The reason for the author's bringing the grim picture of the sufferings of the soul to such a climax is explained by the lines that follow.

But if the ceremonies in honor of Srōsh are celebrated, the angel Srōsh keeps watch over the soul. If the ceremony is performed for one day only, the angel Srōsh protects the soul simply for that period; if it is performed for two days, the protection afforded by Srōsh is for that period only; and if it is performed for all the days, the angel Srōsh protects the soul during all those days.' [50]

Before we conclude this section, we may briefly add a unique allusion found in the Rivāyat of Shāhpūr Barūchī, which pictures the soul as growing from infancy to manhood during the three nights:—

On the first day (after death) the size of the soul is like that of a newly born infant. On the second day the soul grows to the size of a child at the age of seven.[51] On the third day the size of the soul becomes as that of an adult [52] at the age of fifteen.[53]

Following the Pahlavi Dātastān i Dēnīk,[54] the Sad Dar Bundahish and the Rivāyat of Kāmā Bahrā inform us that the soul of the righteous does not feel any pain or misery when the corporeal body is destroyed after death.[55]

[50] RivDH. vol. 1, p. 148 (= Gujarati vers. p. 347); cf. also p. 151 and especially SDBd. 49. 1–10 (= ed. Dhabhar, p. 120–121).

[51] A Parsi child is generally invested with the sacred shirt and girdle at the age of seven (the Navjōt ceremony) and is thus initiated into the Zoroastrian fold. Cf. Vd. 15. 45; Dk., ed. Sanjana, vol. 4, ch. 170 (Eng. tr. p. 263).

[52] According to the Avesta both men and women come of age at fifteen. Cf. Yt. 8. 13, 14; 14. 17; Ys. 9. 5.

[53] RivDH. vol. 1, p. 147 (= Gujarati vers. p. 346).

[54] See above, pages 16–17.

[55] SDBd. 24. 1 (= ed. Dhabhar, p. 93); RivDH. vol. 1, p. 148 (= Gujarati vers. p. 349).

CHAPTER III

THE SOUL OF THE WICKED DURING THE FIRST THREE NIGHTS AFTER DEATH

I

The soul of the wicked in the Later Avesta. In accordance with the Zoroastrian fondness for symmetry, the experience of the soul of the wicked, as it lingers in anguish near the body, is the exact opposite in every detail to that of the righteous soul. The description given in the H a d h ō k h t N a s k is as follows:—

> Zarathushtra asked Ahura Mazdāh: 'O Ahura Mazdāh, most holy Spirit, Creator of the material world, Thou Holy One! When a wicked one dies,[1] where does his soul abide that night?'
>
> Ahura Mazdāh answered: 'There, indeed, in the vicinity of the head, O holy Zarathushtra, it runs about chanting the words of the Kimā Gāthā: "Unto what land, Ahura Mazdāh, shall I go to flee,[2] whither to flee?"[3] On that night his soul experiences as much

---

[1] The Avesta employs a different set of words to describe things and actions when connected with Ahrimanian creatures, to which category the wicked belong. The head of the righteous is *vaγδana*, while that of the wicked is *kamərəδa*; the righteous 'passes away' (*raēθ-*), while the wicked 'dies' (*mar-*); and so forth. See Frachtenberg, 'Ormazdian and Ahrimanian words in Avestan,' in *Spiegel Memorial Volume*, p. 269–289, Bombay, 1908; and H. Güntert, *Über die ahurischen und daēvischen Ausdrücke im Awesta*, Heidelberg, 1914 (*Sitzungsberichte der Heidelberger Akademie der Wissenschaften*, Phil.-hist. Klasse, 1914, 13. Abhandlung); cf. also Moulton, *EZ*. p. 218–219.

[2] *nəmōi . . . nəme*, inf. 'to evade, flee.' Phl. vers. *pa nyāᵛišn* is wrong. See Bthl. *AirWb*. 1071.

[3] The opening line of Ys. 46, beginning with the words *kąm nəmōi ząm*. The Kimā Gāthā is the last section of the second Gāthā. The line quoted in HN. is a rendering of the original Gāthic into Later Avestan, which also adds the words 'Ahura Mazdāh.' The selection of this particular section as

unhappiness as all that which (he experienced as) a living being.'

'Where does his soul abide on the second night?'

Ahura Mazdāh answered: 'There, indeed, in the vicinity of the head, O holy Zarathushtra, it runs about chanting the words of the Kimā Gāthā: "Unto what land, Ahura Mazdāh, shall I go to flee, whither to flee?" On that night his soul experiences as much unhappiness as all that which (he experienced as) a living being.'

'Where does his soul abide on the third night?'

Ahura Mazdāh answered: 'There, indeed, in the vicinity of the head, O holy Zarathushtra, it runs about chanting the words of the Kimā Gāthā: "Unto what land, Ahura Mazdāh, shall I go to flee, whither to flee?" On that night his soul experiences as much unhappiness as all that which (he experienced as) a living being.' [4]

Thus during the first, second, and third nights after death the soul of the wicked cries aloud the Wail of Woe, the Gāthā of lamentation, which begins with the verse *kąm nəmōi ząm kuθrā nəmōi ayenī*.

The cause of these lamentations of the soul is obvious. Besides the mental anguish suffered on account of a life spent in sin, there is the prospect of the impending doom at the Chinvat Bridge [5] and meanwhile, we may suppose, the attack by the

the Wail of Woe is as appropriate as is the choice of Ys. 43 for the Song of Salvation.

It is to be observed that the fifteenth chapter of the Sūtkar Nask was a commentary on Ys. 46. The summary of this chapter is given in the Dēnkart (bk. 9. 16 = *SBE*. 37. 199–204), of which sections 1 and 2 deal with the proceedings of the demon of death; § 3 records that the soul alone sees the events of the spiritual state; and §§ 4–8 are concerned with the treatment of the corpse and the misery of the consciousness. See also *SBE*. 37. 276–282 367–370.

[4] HN. 2 (= Yt. 22). 19–24.
[5] See below, pages 55, 70.

demons of destruction, Vīzaresha and his foul associates Astō-vīdhātu and Vayu.[6] Such is the first step in the triumph of the Evil Spirit and his fiendish hosts over the lost soul as it hovers for three nights near its fleshly dwelling.

II

The soul of the wicked in Pahlavi literature. The Avestan passages cited above are fully supported by the Pahlavi books and are supplemented by the later Persian writings.

The Artāk Vīrāz Nāmak narrates how Saint Vīrāz, after completing his journey to the realms of the pious dead, came back to the Chinvat Bridge accompanied by his heavenly guides Srōsh and Ātar, who granted him a vision of the lot of the wicked. This time he saw the soul of a sinful man, and was informed of the terrible tortures it had undergone during the three nights after death. The description [7] is practically the same as that found in the Hadhōkht Nask, and need not be repeated here.

The account of the fate of the sinful during the three nights, as given in the Pahlavi Rivāyat, is also more or less identical with that of the Hadhōkht Nask. The only additional point to be noted is that it depicts the wicked soul as wrapped in torn and stinking rags (*vastrak i darītak u pūtak*).[8]

The Dātastān i Mēnūk i Khrat, or 'Ordinances of the Spirit of Wisdom,' further states that all the sins and crimes committed by a person in his lifetime are now seen by him with his own eyes during these three days and nights.[9]

According to another Pahlavi work, the Dātastān i Dēnīk, the wicked soul, during the three nights, vividly beholds all the sin it has committed in this life. As in the case of the righteous, it is doubtful at first about its own destination, but soon realizing

[6] For the Avestan passages cf. page 12, above, notes 12-15.
[7] AVN. 17. 1-9.
[8] PhlRiv. 23. 18-21 (= PhlHN. 2. 19-24); cf. ed. Dhabhar, p. 85-86.
[9] MX. 2. 158-160.

the situation, it experiences grievous dread regarding its final accounting and the terrors that await it at the crossing of the Chinvat Bridge, which only anticipate the horrors of Hell.[10] The account continues:—

> On the first night the soul becomes restless on account of its own evil thoughts, on the second night on account of its own evil words, and on the third night on account of its own evil deeds; but owing to the good works which it has done in the world, the Spirit of (its) Good Thoughts (*mēnūk i hūmēnišnīh*) comes to the soul on the first night, the Spirit of Good Words (*mēnūk i hūgōvišnīh*) on the second night, and the Spirit of Good Deeds (*mēnūk i hūkūnišnīh*) on the third night, and the soul becomes happy and courageous.[11]

Thus the soul of the wicked, if not absolutely immersed in sin, receives a certain amount of recompense for such works of merit as it may have performed in this world. The sufferings of the spirit during those three nights are thus made somewhat more bearable.

The Bundahishn in its Indian recension speaks of the demon Vīzār(ē)sh and how he struggles with the souls of men doomed to perdition, carrying them away terror-stricken.[12] The account which the text gives is similar to that found in the Vidēvdāt, as already noted. The Iranian Bundahishn, however, which is in general fuller, describes the wicked soul as lamenting thus:—

> 'With the body, while life was still within the body,
> I have wandered a wandering (*bē dōbārišn dōbārēt*

[10] DD. 25. 1, 2.
[11] DD. 25. 4. As in the case of the righteous, the author of the book assumes that the wicked are not altogether wicked. They too may have performed some good actions in the course of their life, and are justified in receiving some consideration. Cf. above, page 15.
[12] Bd. 28. 18.

hōm).¹³ To what place¹⁴ shall I flee at last from here?'¹⁵

Thus the soul of the wicked cherishes the vain hope that by some miracle it may re-enter the body in order to have a chance to make up for the sins committed during its life on earth.

The account given in the Dātastān i Dēnīk matches exactly with the point brought out above in the passage from the Iranian Bundahishn. Thus it states that when the soul of the wicked sees the body being destroyed 'it becomes desirous of its bodily existence once more' and utters a cry of repentance thus:—

> 'During my bodily existence and worldly progress, why did I not atone for my sins? Why did I not accumulate merits? . . . With this body, it would have been possible for me to atone for sin (and thus) to release (bōxtan) the soul, but now I am separated from everything—the joy of the material world and the great hope of the spiritual world; and I have attained to (i.e. I am subjected to) the severe accounting and to greater danger.'¹⁶

As it utters these words, realizing that the chance for escape from perdition is lost for all time, the destruction of the body causes great grief and misery to the soul.¹⁷

And now we turn once more to the question of the commendatory ceremonies. So far as our present knowledge of the Gāthās and the Later Avesta goes,¹⁸ the performance of rites,

---

[13] The auxiliary hōm with passive past participle forms the perfect. Modi takes it with the sentence following, and reads it as hōmanam 'in the sense of azəm.'

[14] Ys. 46. 1, quoted with slight variation.

[15] IrBd. 30. 3. (Cf. Anklesaria, p. 200, facsimile edition of ms.)

[16] DD. 16. 4; contrast pages 16–17, above.

[17] DD. 16. 5; cf. also Dk. 9. 16. 8, and PhlRiv. 24. 1–2 (= ed. Dhabhar, p. 89–90).

[18] In the light of these writings, we can safely say that death ends the state of probation, i.e. after death man can no longer acquire either merit or demerit.

even during the first three nights after death, would be a mere act of supererogation in the case of the righteous, while it would seem to be altogether unavailing in the case of the wicked. As already noted, the Pahlavi and later Persian writings emphasize greatly the importance of the celebration of these ceremonies in honor of the angel Srōsh, as enabling him to guard the soul against the onslaughts of the evil powers, but they fail to show how the wicked could thereby claim his protection. In the absence of explicit statements, we can at least fancy from the spirit of these later texts that such ceremonies, which are considered to be indispensable in the case of a departed soul, are not only helpful as strengthening and gladdening the righteous but may prove a source of comfort even to the wicked.[19]

III

The soul of the wicked in Parsi-Persian literature. Turning now to the New Persian Zoroastrian writings of the Parsis, the Sad Dar Bundahish, in discussing the fate of the wicked soul during the first three nights, briefly describes how the soul feels terrible pain when the body is disposed of, uttering words of woe and repentance for bringing upon itself eternal damnation through its own evil thoughts, words, and deeds; and, wailing bitterly, it rebukes the body it once inhabited, in the following words:—

(4) 'O the coward (nā javānmard) that thou art! When the manly ones (mardān)[20] sought duty and good works, thou soughtest property and wealth (māl u xᵛāsta), that (thy) sons, daughters, and relatives might enjoy and squander! And thou didst not do any good work for my sake, who am the soul, and didst not accumulate (na andūxtī) any merit (čīz i beh) which may come to my assistance.

[19] Cf. DD. chaps. 8–13, and especially Āfrīn i Artāk Fravart 14.
[20] Better read thus; all mss. have murādān.

(5) Now the relatives are not performing any duty and good works on our behalf; and the property and (the fruit) of thy labors which thou didst earn and lay up, these they (i.e. relatives) are now squandering; and they do not consecrate the sacred cake (*drōn*) on our behalf. On account of thy doings (*kardār*) I shall fall in torment (*'aẓāb*) and punishment (*'uqūbat*) and retribution (*pādafrāh*) till the Resurrection (*ristaxīz*) and the future body (*tan i pasīn*).'

Thus repenting and rebuking, bewailing and bemoaning its wretched lot, the soul of the wicked proceeds on its journey to the world beyond on the dawn of the fourth day after death.[21] Such, in brief, is the sorrowful experience of the wicked soul during the first three days and nights, while it hovers about the body.

[21] SDBd. 24. 2–8 (ed. Dhabhar, p. 93–94). The whole chapter is quoted, though without mention of the fact, in the Rivāyat of Kāmā Bahrā; see RivDH. vol. 1, p. 148–149 (= Gujarati vers. p. 349–350).

CHAPTER IV

THE MANIFESTATION OF THE DAĒNĀ, OR CONSCIENCE, TO THE SOUL, ACCORDING TO THE GĀTHĀS

Introduction: discussion of the term Daēnā. The concept of the Daēnā, or Conscience, and the role it plays in determining man's destiny hereafter, is one of Zarathushtra's fundamental doctrines and forms a keynote of his eschatological teachings in the Gāthās.

The technical term *daēnā* has been variously interpreted by scholars, and consequently calls for comment. The writer is inclined to believe that there are two distinct concepts in this word. In the first place, it is used objectively in the sense of 'religion' in numerous passages both in the Gāthās and in the Later Avesta.[1] What we are chiefly concerned with here is the other and more subjective sense, which Bartholomae would render as 'inner being, spiritual ego, individuality' (inneres Wesen, geistiges Ich, Individualität).[2] A number of scholars, following his view, have understood the word as 'ego' or 'self.'[3]

[1] Bthl. *AirWb.* 662–665, s.v. ¹ *daēnā-*. Bartholomae makes two separate entries, as if there were two etymologically distinct words, but this seems improbable, even if no satisfactory etymology for *daēnā-* has yet been proposed. See Persson, *Beitr. zur idg. Wortforschung*, p. 717–718; Autran, *Sumérien et Indo-Européen*, p. 153; Oliphant, *JAOS.* 32. 412–413.

[2] Bthl. *AirWb.* 665–667, s.v. ² *daēnā-*. Bartholomae explains more fully in his footnote (here rendered from the German) as follows: 'A theologico-philosophical concept, the totality of the psychic and religious characteristics of a person, his psychic and religious individuality. It lives on after his death as an independent being (cf. under *fravašay-*), so as finally to accompany the one who has risen again (or his soul) to Paradise or Hell, after it had appeared to him (or to his soul) in the form of a beautiful or a hideous maiden, as a reflection, so to speak, of his inner being.'

[3] Thus Reitzenstein, *Das iran. Erlösungsmysterium*, p. 31–32, 39, 48, renders *daēnā* as 'Ich (Person, Selbst)'; Moulton, *EZ.* p. xii, 162, 171, 179, 263–265, 278, 310, 353, 368 as 'self,' but p. 265, 268, 432 as 'Religion'; and latest (1925) Meillet, *Trois Conférences sur les Gāthā*, p. 57–58, gives the

It seems to the writer, however, that such an interpretation fails to bring to the minds of the readers the full import of the term.

The author's own feeling is that what Zoroaster meant, in his highly spiritualized way of thinking, was summed up by Jackson years ago, when he rendered the graphic image as 'the Conscience, or Religion personified.'[4] Geldner likewise holds a similar view, taking *daēnā* either as 'Religion' or 'Religious Conscience.'[5]

The present writer, on the whole, believes that the conception of religious insight connoted by the term *daēnā* is best expressed by 'Conscience,' and he has accordingly adopted this rendering in preference to 'ego' or 'self.'

The office of the Daēnā in the Gāthās. As intimated already,[6] the Gāthās lay special stress on the doctrine that a man's Conscience (*daēnā*)[7] is the real determinant of his future destiny. Man is endowed with free will. Though helped by the teachings of the Prophet, which are the revelation of the good laws of Mazdāh, it is left entirely to man to make a free

compromise rendering as 'personnalité religieuse.' Consult also Wesendonk, *Urmensch und Seele*, p. 198–200.

[4] In *Biblical World*, 8. 154, Chicago, 1896 (reprinted in E. H. Sneath's *Religion and the Future Life*, p. 127). Darmesteter also translated *daēnā* as 'conscience' in *SBE*. (cf. vol. 23, p. 315, etc.), but later changed it to 'Religion' in *ZA*. (cf. vol. 2, p. 652, etc.), the latter term being employed both by Söderblom, *La Vie future*, p. 8, etc., and by Böklen, *Pars. Eschatologie*, p. 19, etc.

[5] See *Theologische Literaturzeitung*, 1922, no. 6, p. 125, where Geldner reviews Reitzenstein's *Das iranische Erlösungsmysterium*. In discussing the term *daēnā* Geldner sums up his opinion concisely in the following words (here translated from the German): 'Daena is always "religion," either religion as the sum of the articles of faith, as the "Mazda-worshiping daena," or subjectively the religion of the individual, his religious conscience. In this way the well-known allegory becomes intelligible according to which the soul's Daena, i.e. its conscience, meets it after death in the form of a beautiful maiden. Later presentations of this allegory substitute for this the individual's good works, which, as is well known, are stored up in Heaven. The role which Zarathushtra himself causes the Daena to play at the Bridge of Judgment corresponds to this.'

[6] See above, page 28.

[7] The *daēnā* (conscience) is expressly distinguished from the *urvan* (soul); cf., for example, Ys. 45. 2. According to Ys. 31. 11 and 46. 6, Mazdāh created man's *daēnā* at the beginning of his life on earth.

choice between the Two Principles, the warring kingdoms of Good and Evil.[8] It is 'the wise' (*hudā̊ŋhō*) who choose aright,[9] and who, by their good thoughts, words, and deeds, acquire merit in this life and felicity in the life hereafter. 'The foolish' (*duždā̊ŋhō*), on the other hand, do not choose rightly,[9] but, yielding to the temptation of evil thoughts, words, and deeds, bring misery upon themselves in the present world and damnation in the next. In either case, it is man's own Conscience which leads his soul either to eternal bliss or to everlasting perdition:—

> Whoso comes over to the Righteous One,[10] removed [11] afar from him hereafter shall be the long duration of misery, of darkness, foul food, and woful words.[12] To such a life, O ye wicked, shall your Daēnā (Conscience) lead you through your own deeds.[13]

The man of Good Thought, who takes the correct side in the battle between the Two Principles, and who uses the right weapon, his is the 'happiness' (*īžā*) and that 'satisfying fulness' (*āzūitiš*) which are to be found in this world and the other:—

> He, O Mazdāh, is happiness and fulness (personified), whosoever has united his Daēnā (Conscience) with Vohu Manah, being well cognizant [14] of Armaiti through Asha, and with all those in Thy Kingdom, O Ahura.[15]

---

[8] Ys. 30. 2, 3; 31. 11, 12.
[9] Ys. 30. 3.
[10] Referring undoubtedly to Zarathushtra himself.
[11] Thus taking *divamnəm* from * *dū-* or ² *dav-*, 'remove.' See Geldner in BB. 14. 13; Bthl. *AirWb*. 747.
[12] Literally, 'woe of speech.'
[13] Ys. 31. 20. Cf. Vd. 5. 62, which paraphrases the last verse.
[14] *hu-zə̄ntav-*; Phl. vers. has *xup šnāsak*; see Bthl. *AirWb*. 1839.
[15] Ys. 49. 5. Cf. also Ys. 34. 13; 44. 9; 45. 11; 49. 9; 51. 17, 21; 53. 4; 54. 1; and note also (in the Yasna Haptanghāiti) Ys. 39. 2; 40. 1; and 41. 5. These latter eschatological passages (though touching on the Daēnā doctrine, yet not directly bearing on the subject here) are reserved for presentation at some future time.

But the man of Bad Thought will mar his own future, and his Conscience will torment him and will bring him to hell through his own sinful deeds:—

> But as for the wicked, who belong to the Kingdom of Evil, who have evil deeds, evil words, evil Daēnā (Conscience), and evil thought—the souls [16] will come to meet them with foul food; they will be veritable inmates in the House of the Lie.[17]
>
> Through their power the Karpans [18] and the Kavis [19] have yoked [20] man up with evil deeds in order to destroy his (future) life—but [21] their own soul and their own Conscience (Daēnā) will cause them anguish when they come where the Chinvat Bridge is, to be dwellers in the House of the Druj for all eternity.[22]
>
> Therefore the Daēnā of the wicked destroys the verity of the Right Way for him, and his (*yehyā*) soul will suffer anguish at the Judgment [23] of the Chinvat Bridge, having strayed from the Path of Asha through his own deeds and tongue.[24]

As to the fate of the wavering man, who makes his own Daēnā now better, now worse, we read as follows:—

---

[16] This refers to the souls of the *drəgvant* who have died earlier and preceded them to the House of the Lie.

[17] Ys. 49. 11.

[18] A name of the priests of the *daēvayasna*; cf. Skt. *kalpa*, 'ritual.'

[19] A name of the *daēvayasna* chiefs, when used separately.

[20] Bthl., *AirWb.* 1229, renders *yūfən* as 'accustom to' (gewöhnen . . . an) with instrumental.

[21] *yə̄ng* to be resolved into conjunction plus demonstr. pron., 'but . . . them.'

[22] Ys. 46. 11; see later, page 59, note 64.

[23] *ākā̊*, 'judgment, revelation, manifestation, laying open of the way,' etc.; see Bthl. *AirWb.* 309.

[24] Ys. 51. 13, see also page 55, below.

He who, O Mazdāh, makes his thought now better, now worse, and thereby his Daēnā through deed and word, who follows his own wishes, desires, and beliefs, he will be a p a r t (in a Separate Place) [25] at the last in accordance with Thy determination.[26]

[25] The stanza quoted refers to the concept of the Hamistakān; see below, p. 50. The word *nanā* is an adverb; Bthl. *AirWb*. 1041.
[26] Ys. 48. 4.

CHAPTER V

THE MANIFESTATION OF THE DAĒNĀ, OR CONSCIENCE, TO THE SOUL, ACCORDING TO THE LATER AVESTA

Introduction. Wholly in the spirit of the Gāthās is the beautiful conception of these later scriptural writings, according to which the Conscience, or Religion personified,[1] comes to greet the soul at the dawn of the fourth day after death, either in the form of a lovely maiden, or in the shape of a hideous hag. The maiden appears amid a breath of balmy wind, fragrant with scents and perfumes; the hag arrives amid the chill of a foul blast heavy with sickening stench.

I

The Daēnā greets the soul of the righteous. The striking picture of the blissful state of the righteous soul and its pleasant experiences, as presented in the fragment of the Hadhōkht Nask, is as follows:—

(7) At the end [2] of the third night, when the dawn appears,[3] the soul of the righteous man seems to be among plants, and to be inhaling [4] fragrant odors. There seems to blow towards him, from the regions of

---

[1] The *daēnā* is one of the five spiritual faculties or constituents of man, which are *ahū* (life), *daēnā* (conscience), *baoδah* (consciousness), *urvan* (soul), and *fravašay* (Fravashi), as mentioned in Ys. 26. 4; Yt. 13. 149, 155; HN. 1. 4; cf. Bthl. *AirWb.* 283, 666, 919, 1538, 992. Dr. Dhalla's statement (in *Zoroastrian Theology*, p. 176) that the *daēnā* is the only spiritual faculty besides the soul of which we hear anything after the dissolution of the body, is not correct. It is natural that there can be no reference to the *ahū*, but the remaining four are repeatedly mentioned in the Avesta in this connection; cf. the passages given by Bartholomae on the pages cited above. See also above, page 9, note 1.

[2] Literally, 'at the completion.'

[3] Literally, 'it seems to be dawning, illucescere videtur'; Bthl. *AirWb.* 1479.

[4] *vīdiδārəmnō* ([3] *dar*-), 'receiving'; see Bthl. *AirWb.* 692.

34 THE MANIFESTATION OF THE DAĒNĀ

the south,[5] a wind fragrant, more fragrant than all others.

(8) And the soul of this righteous man seems to inhale [6] this wind with the nose, (and reflects): 'Whence blows the wind, which is the most fragrant wind I ever inhaled with my nostrils?'

(9) At the approach [7] of this wind, there appears to him his own Conscience in the form of a Maiden,[8] beautiful, radiant, white-armed, robust, fair-faced, erect,[9] high-breasted, of stately form, noble-born, of glorious lineage, fifteen years old in appearance (*pančadasayå raoδaēšva*), as beautiful in form as the most beautiful of creatures.

(10) And the soul of the righteous man addressed her, asking: 'What damsel art thou, the most beautiful of damsels in form whom I have ever seen?'

(11a) Then to him his own Conscience gave answer: 'O thou youth of Good Thought, Good Word, Good Deed, of Good Conscience, I am the Conscience of thine own self.' [10]

(11b) [The youth speaks:] 'And who is it that hath loved [11] thee for that majesty, goodness, beauty, fragrance, victorious might, and power to overcome the foe as thou appearest unto me?' [12]

---

[5] That is, from the southernmost region, where Heaven is situated, according to Zoroastrianism.

[6] *uz-grəmbayō* (pres. part. act. from *grab-*), 'drawing in'; Bthl. *AirWb.* 528.

[7] *frōrənta*, loc. sg.; Bthl. *AirWb.* 1023.

[8] The description of the Maiden given here is somewhat similar to that of the goddess *Arədvī Sūrā* in Yt. 5. 64, 78, 126.

[9] Reading *uz-arštayå* as in ms. K20; cf. Bthl. *AirWb.* 410; Darmesteter, *ZA.* 2. 653, prefers *hu-zarštayå*, rendering by 'droite' (lit. 'bien tirée'), comparing *ni-zarəšaiti*.

[10] Lit. 'the own (*hava*) Conscience of (thine) own person ($x^v a\bar{e}pai\theta e.tanvō$, gen. sg.).'

[11] *čakana* (^{1} *kan-*), perf. 3d singular.

[12] Observe particularly that in this instance the Phl. vers. correctly divides the sentences, separating *čišča . . . saδayehi* from the preceding one. So also Geldner, *Religionsgeschichtliches Lesebuch*, p. 353, thus putting these

(12) [The Maiden answers:] 'O youth of good thought, good word, good deed, of good conscience, it is thou that hast loved [13] me for such majesty, goodness, beauty, fragrance, victorious might, and power to overcome the foe as I appear unto thee.

(13) When thou sawest another performing burning (i.e. of the dead) [14] and idol-worship,[15] and causing oppression,[16] and cutting down trees,[17] then thou wouldst sit down, chanting the Gāthās, and sacrificing to the good waters and the fire of Ahura Mazdāh, and befriending [18] the pious man coming from near and from afar.

(14) So me, being lovable, (thou madest) still more lovable; me, being beautiful, (thou madest) still more beautiful; me, being desirable, (thou madest) still more desirable; me, sitting in a high place, (thou madest) sitting in a still higher place.' [19]

---

words in the mouth of the 'youth' and not of the 'Conscience.' This seems correct and logical. The second inquiry on the part of the 'youth' likewise begins with the word *čišča* as in the first instance. Haug and West, *Bk. of AV.*, Append. 2, p. 311, and Darmesteter, *SBE.* 23. 316 = *ZA.* 2. 653, connect this stanza with the preceding as part of the Damsel's utterance.

[13] *čakana* here wrongly 3d sg. instead of 2d sg., the form having been taken over from the preceding stanza.

[14] *saočaya-*, 'burning,' so also Geldner and Haug; but Darmesteter gives 'derision' (of holy things), following Phl. vers. *afsūs*. Bthl., *AirWb.* 1550, avoids translating the word definitely.

[15] *baosav-*, cf. Haug and West, p. 312, but doubted by Bthl., *AirWb.* 920. Geldner does not translate this word, nor the following. Consult likewise Darmesteter, *ZA.* 2. 653, on the conjectural rendering as 'idolâtrie.'

[16] *varaxəδrāsča varōžintəm* (rendered conjecturally); see also Haug and West, p. 312; Darmesteter, *ZA.* 2. 653, 'qui refusait la charité'; Bthl. *AirWb.* 1367 (not translated, but Phl. vers. cited). The form *varōžintəm* is possibly miswritten for *vərəzintəm*; cf. Bthl. *AirWb.* 1377 n. 5 (1376 [1] *varəz-*, and 1366 *varō.jinō*).

[17] Darmesteter differently, 'mettait son blé sous la clef.'

[18] *kuxšnvqnō* ([1] *xšnav-*), 'satisfying, propitiating, extolling, befriending,' i.e. giving hospitality to strangers.

[19] HN. 2. 7-14 (= VYt. 55-60). The remaining two sentences of § 14 are the words of Ahura Mazdāh and are correctly designated as such by

36 THE MANIFESTATION OF THE DAĒNĀ

According to the description given in the Vidēvdāt, two dogs, guarding the soul from demons, accompany the figure of the Maiden [20]:—

> She (namely, the Maiden), beautifully formed, strong, fair-faced, comes with the dogs at her side,[21] wearing a bodice (*nivavaiti*) [22] and a crown (*pusavaiti*),[23] dextrous (*yaoxštivaiti*) and skilful (*hunaravaiti*). . . .[24]
> She leads the souls of the righteous across the lofty Harā, she supports them across the Chinvat Bridge on that span [25] (leading) to the spiritual Yazatas (angels).[26]

The account in the Vidēvdāt, as given above, differs from that in the Hadhōkht Nask (2. 7–14) and its counterpart in the Vishtāsp Yasht (55–60) not only in the description of the lovely Maiden herself, but also as to the part she plays in guiding Geldner. On the other hand, Haug and West, p. 313, seem to take them as spoken by the Maiden.

[20] This seems to be a rifacimento of an old Indo-Iranian belief. Cf. also Vd. 13. 9, where the dogs guard the Chinvat Bridge; see below, p. 70, n. 54.

[21] Gray (*Le Muséon*, nouv. série, 3, p. 155) offers a new translation of *spānavaiti* and the two Avestan words that follow, as 'beneficent (?), stout (?), keen-sighted (?).' In support of his proposed rendering he gives etymological reasons in the footnote.

[22] A difficult word. Geldner, 'Brusttuch' in *Rel.-gesch. Lesebuch*, p. 354; Bthl., *AirWb.* 1084, does not translate it; Phl. vers. *vičārišnōmand*, 'discriminating,' followed by Darmesteter. In some of the Avestan mss. this word is omitted. Compare the description of the apparel and garments of *Arədvī Sūrā*, as given in Yt. 5. 126–131.

[23] Thus Geldner, *op. cit.* p. 354. For *pusā-* f., 'diadem, crown,' see Bthl. *AirWb.* 911. Bthl., *AirWb.* 884, prefers to read here the variant *pasvaiti*, but leaves the interpretation open.

[24] For a discussion of the sentence here omitted in translation see p. 65, n. 33.

[25] Literally, 'on the bridgeway of the spiritual Yazatas.' Av. *haētav-* (Skt. *setu*) is a synonym of *pərətav-*. The loc. sg. is interpreted by Geldner and Bartholomae as practically meaning 'to the landing stage.' The verb *vīδārayeiti* appropriately pictures the support given to the righteous soul to prevent it from falling into Hell.

[26] Vd. 19. 30.

the soul's celestial journey. According to the Vidēvdāt she conducts the soul of the righteous to the Judgment Seat at the Chinvat Bridge, and after the decision is formally pronounced on the happy soul, she makes it cross the Bridge happily and triumphantly.

II

The Daēnā meets the Soul of the Wicked. Turning now to the distressing experiences endured by the wicked, the fragment of the Hadhōkht Nask, previously cited, gives the following description:—

> (25) At the end of the third night, O holy Zarathushtra, when the dawn appears, the soul of the wicked man seems to be amid frosts [27] and to be inhaling stenches. There seems to blow towards him from the region of the north, from the regions of the north,[28] a wind foul-smelling—more foul-smelling than all others.
>
> (26) And the soul of this wicked man seems to inhale this wind with the nose, (and reflects): 'Whence blows the wind, which is the foulest wind I ever inhaled with my nostrils?' [29]

Immediately after this scene there should follow the description of the dreadful Hag, as we know from the Pahlavi passages quoted below. This is omitted in the Avestan text itself, but its contents, as being the converse of HN. 2. 9–14, could easily be restored from those sources.

[27] Read *aēxāhu* with Darmesteter, *ZA*. 2. 656 n. 29, followed by Bthl. *AirWb*. 11, where this emendation is supported. We may add that one of the Pahlavi accounts of hell itself (cf. MX. 7. 27) includes a region that is 'cold as the coldest,' etc. Geldner, however, keeps the reading *aēiθāhu* and translates as 'in einer Wüstenei,' contrasting the idea of a wilderness with *urvarāhu* (cf. HN. 2. 7).

[28] That is, the northernmost region, where Hell is situated, according to Zoroastrianism. Cf. Vd. 19. 1; MX. 49. 15–17.

[29] HN. 2. 25–26.

THE MANIFESTATION OF THE DAĒNĀ

We can possibly infer from our Vidēvdāt account that instead of the ugly Hag, as we might expect, it is the foul demon Vīzaresha who drags the soul of the wicked to the Seat of Judgment at the Chinvat Bridge, whence, after the verdict has been rendered, he carries the damned spirit to the dark abyss of Hell:—

> (29) The demon Vīzaresha [30] by name, O Spitama Zarathushtra, leads away in bonds [31] the soul of the wicked, the lost-life [32] of the demon-worshiping men . . . to the Chinvat Bridge created by Mazdāh . . .
>
> (30b) . . . He [33] (namely Vīzaresha) drags down (*nizaršaite*) the sinful [34] souls of the wicked to Darkness (i.e. to Hell).[35]

[30] See above, page 24, and cf. below, page 63, note 21.
[31] Cf. below, page 63, note 22.
[32] Cf. below, page 64, note 23.
[33] See below, page 65, note 31.
[34] See below, page 65, note 32.
[35] Vd. 19. 29–30. See especially page 65, note 33.

CHAPTER VI

THE MANIFESTATION OF THE DAĒNĀ, OR CONSCIENCE, TO THE SOUL, ACCORDING TO THE PAHLAVI AND PARSI-PERSIAN LITERATURE

I

The Daēnā greets the righteous soul. According to the account given in the Dātastān i Mēnūk i Khrat, the soul of the righteous commences its journey to the great beyond with the help of the powers of Good, but not without facing opposition and impediments thrown in its way by the powers of Evil. The latter are ever eager to drag it to Hell, without making any distinction whether it be a righteous or a wicked soul, and without waiting for the trial which it must undergo at the Judgment Seat before its destiny is determined.[1]

This book [2] gives a detailed description of the meeting of the soul of the righteous with its own Conscience in the form of a beautiful damsel (*kanīk*) personifying its own good deeds. The account is nearly identical with that already found in the Hadhōkht Nask, and need not be repeated. But before we pass on, it would be well to observe in this connection that according to this Pahlavi text [3] the Daēnā greets the soul after the Judgment is rendered instead of before.

The accounts given in the Artāk Vīrāz Nāmak [4] and in the Pahlavi Rivāyat [5] are also similar to that of the Hadhōkht Nask, and do not require repetition here.

The notable Pahlavi book Dēnkart gives a brief description of the Daēnā as appearing to the soul of a righteous man. She

---

[1] MX. 2. 115; cf. also Aog. 8–9. For a fuller discussion of the subject see below, pages 83–84.
[2] MX. 2. 125–144; cf. also later SDBd. 99. 5–12; see below, pages 44–45.
[3] Cf. also IrBd. 30. 11; see below, page 93.
[4] AVN. 4. 15–36.
[5] PhlRiv. 23. 5–12 (= PhlHN. 2. 7–14); ed. Dhabhar, p. 82–83.

comes, as before, in the form of a beautiful maiden (*hūčihr kanīk*) who conducts the soul into Paradise.[6]

The Dātastān i Dēnīk and the Shkand-vimānīk Vichār also narrate how the Maiden comes on the dawn of the fourth day to greet the soul 'with the store of its own merits,' and in this description she is called 'the treasurer of merits.' [7]

According to the Iranian Bundahishn, in addition to the manifestation of the Maiden to the soul of the righteous amid a fair wind, there also appear before it a fat cow and an enchanting garden:—

> (4) And if (the soul be that of) a righteous man, immediately with those words [8] there comes toward it a wind that is better <more excellent> and more fragrant <more auspicious> than all the winds that are in the world, and it pleases the soul . . .[9]
>
> (5) . . . Then there comes before it on the way the form of a cow (*gāv*), fat and full of milk, from which happiness and sweetness come to the soul.
>
> Secondly,[10] there comes before it the form of a Maiden (*kanīk*), a beautiful form in white raiment and fifteen years of age, who is fair from every side (*hač hamah kōstak*), and at whom the soul is pleased.[11]
>
> Thirdly,[10] there comes the form of a garden (*bōstān*), full of fresh fruits (*pūr-bar*), full of water (*pūr-āp*), full of dried fruits (*pūr-mīwak*), and full of fertility (*pūr-patixū*), from which come joyous and happy thoughts to the soul. This is a heavenly place, which it sees before the accounting (*pīš hač hamār*) as a sign (*daxšak*)

---

[6] Dk., ed. Sanjana, vol. 2, text, p. 74–75, tr. p. 82.
[7] DD. 24. 5; ŠVV. 4. 91–96; see below, page 73.
[8] That is, with the utterance of the Song of Salvation; see above, p. 13.
[9] IrBd. 30. 4; cf. also Modi, in *JBBRAS*. 21. 59.
[10] *dit . . . dit*, as an adj. 'the other . . . the other'; as an adv. 'secondly . . . thirdly,' which brings out the force of the repetition.
[11] *šātihēt* (passive), and not *shād shayēt* as read by Modi.

in this world [of the attainment of the real Heaven that is near at hand].¹²

(6) Then the soul questions them (i.e. the apparitions) one after the other,¹³ asking: 'Who art thou that pleasest (*sahēt*) me thus <i.e. that art all felicity and comfort>?'

Thereupon they, one by one, answer thus: 'I am the righteous Dēn of thy actions which thou didst perform when thou didst goodness; here was I formed on thy account [such as thou seest me].'¹⁴

II

The Daēnā meets the wicked soul. As noted above, a development similar to that in the Hadhōkht Nask, 9–14, describing the converse picture, the experience of the soul of the wicked and its being met by a hideous old woman, who is its own Daēnā, is preserved in the Artāk Vīrāz Nāmak and the Dātastān i Mēnūk i Khrat. As these two accounts are practically identical, only that from the former need be considered. Nor is it necessary to reproduce here the account given in the Pahlavi Rivāyat, which follows closely that contained in the two above-mentioned Pahlavi works.

The Pahlavi book Artāk Vīrāz Nāmak gives a striking portrait of the appearance of the ugly Hag who meets the lost soul of the wicked, and it records the dialogue that is carried on between them. This is worth translating from the Pahlavi in extenso, as follows:—

(10–11) Afterwards, a stinking cold wind comes across to greet the soul. It seems as if this came forth from the northern region, <from the region of the demons>. A more stinking wind than which, it had not perceived in the world.

---
¹² IrBd. 30. 5; cf. also Modi, *op. cit.* p. 60–61.
¹³ *ēvak ēvak*, lit. 'one by one' (used distributively). Modi has 'one another.'
¹⁴ IrBd. 30. 6; cf. also Modi, *op. cit.* p. 61.

(12) And in that wind it beheld that which was its own Conscience and deeds, as a whore [15] (*zan i Jēh*), naked and decrepit, with exposed thighs in front and buttocks behind,[16] with endless spots <that is, spot was joined to spot>, like the most noxious creatures <most filthy and most stinking>.

(13) And afterwards the soul of the wicked spoke thus: 'Who art thou, than whom, among all the creatures of Ōhrmazd and Aharman, I never saw any uglier (*zīšttar*), filthier, and more stinking?'

(14–15) To it she spoke thus: 'I am thy bad deeds, O youth of evil thought, evil word, evil deed, and of evil Conscience. It is on account of thy will and actions that I am ugly and vile, disgusting and diseased, decrepit and of evil complexion (*duš-gōnak*), unfortunate and distressed, as it seems to thee.

(16–20) When thou sawest another performing the Yazishn and Drōn (ceremonies), and offering praise and prayer and worship to God, and preserving and protecting the water and fire, cattle, trees, and the other good creations, thou didst the will of Aharman and the demons, and didst unlawful deeds. And when thou sawest another giving gifts and performing charity deservedly for the benefit of the good and worthy, and providing hospitable reception to those who came from far and near, thou wast avaricious and didst shut up thy door.

---

[15] This description of the hag, which is no longer extant in the Hadhōkht Nask, as noted above, closely resembles that of the fiend Nasu in Vd. 7. 2; 8. 71; 9. 26. We might safely say that it is borrowed from the Phl. version of the Vidēvdāt, as the same glosses are found in both texts.

[16] *wišātak* (= *vi°*) *i frāj-jānū i awāj-kūn*. Rather bad words, but such is evidently the way in which the Pahlavi writers interpreted the Av. words *frašnaoš apazaδaṅhō* in Vd. 7. 2, etc.; Haug and West translate them as 'gaping, bandy-legged, lean-hipped' (in *Bk. of AV.* p. 167, *Glossary*, p. 104 bottom).

(21–26) And though I was unholy <that is, I was considered bad>, thou didst make me still more unholy [17]; though I was frightful, thou hast made me still more frightful; though I was wavering (*drafšnīk*), thou hast made me still more wavering; though I was sitting in the northern region, thou hast made me sit still farther northward,—through these evil thoughts, through these evil words, and through these evil deeds which thou didst. For long eons (*dēr zamān*) they shall curse me in that which is the long execration and evil communion of the Evil Spirit.' [18]

The Dēnkart informs us similarly that if a person becomes a follower of the Principle of Evil by doing deeds that help sinfulness, the Daēnā appears in the guise of a courtesan (*čarāitīk*),[19] who drags him to Hell.[20] Both the Dātastān i Dēnīk and the Shkand-vimānīk Vichār also furnish the converse picture to that of the lovely damsel, namely, the ghastly form of the courtesan, who is a tormentor and comes to meet the wicked soul with 'the store of its sin.' [21]

In this connection we should particularly notice the Iranian Bundahishn, which supplements its account of the hideous Hag (contrasted with the Maiden) by logically adding a lean cow and a barren garden to offset the figure of the milch-cow and the flourishing vineyard seen by the soul of the righteous. No sooner has the wicked breathed the stench of a foul wind than he beholds these frightful apparitions. They are the grim messengers of the coming retribution; and the soul, filled with anguish, questions each of them in turn as to its significance,

---

[17] The passive construction in the original is here changed to the active form for convenience in translating.

[18] AVN. 17. 10–26, see also Haug and West's translation, p. 167–168; MX. 2. 167–181; PhlRiv. 23. 22–29 (ed. Dhabhar, p. 86–88). Cf. also IrBd. 30. 12; see below, page 93.

[19] See below, page 87, note 81.

[20] Dk., ed. Sanjana, vol. 2, text, p. 74–75, tr. p. 83.

[21] DD. 25. 5; SVV. 4. 91–96; see below, page 73.

learning in answer that each typifies the individual Conscience (*dēn*), evil in thought, word, and deed, as the result of a life of sin in this world.[22]

III

The Daēnā in the Parsi-Persian Literature. The only noteworthy account of the Daēnā contained in these later Zoroastrian writings in Persian is found in the important treatise Sad Dar Bundahish. It describes how the souls of the righteous and of the wicked meet the impersonation of their deeds done on earth, but this meeting is pictured as taking place after judgment has been passed upon the soul and while it is in the act of crossing the Chinvat Bridge.[23] If the soul be that of a righteous man,

> when it takes a step over the Chinvat Bridge, there comes to it a fragrant wind from Paradise, which smells of musk and ambergris (*'anbar*), and that fragrance is more pleasant to it than any other pleasure.
>
> When it reaches the middle of the Bridge, it beholds an apparition (*ṣūrat*) of such beauty that it hath never seen a figure of greater beauty than hers. She approaches it, and (when) it sees that apparition, it is amazed at the purity of that apparition.
>
> And when the apparition appears to the soul at the Chinvat Bridge—the apparition with such beauty and purity—, it smiles and speaks thus: 'Who art thou with such beauty that a figure with greater beauty I have never seen?'
>
> The apparition speaks (thus): 'I am thy own good actions (*kardār i nīk*). I myself was good, but thy actions have made me better.'

[22] IrBd. 30. 4, 7, 8; cf. also Modi, *op. cit.* p. 59–60, 61–62
[23] The situation is therefore similar to that depicted in IrBd. 30. 11–13, cf. below, p. 93, although the dialogue resembles that in the Pahlavi accounts already cited.

And she embraces him, and they both depart with complete joy and ease to Paradise.[24]

But if the soul be that of a sinful man,

when it takes a step over the Chinvat Bridge, there blows to him an exceedingly foul wind from Hell, so foul as is unheard of among all the stench in the world. There is no stench fouler than that; and that stench is the worst of all the punishments that are visited upon it.

When it reaches the middle of the Chinvat Bridge, it sees an apparition (*ṣūrat*) of such extreme ugliness and frightfulness that it hath never seen one uglier and more unseemly than her. And it is as much terrified on account of her as a sheep is of a wolf, and wants to flee away from her.

And that apparition speaks thus: 'Whither dost thou want to flee?'

It (i.e. the soul) speaks thus: 'Who art thou with such ugliness and terror that a figure worse than thou art, uglier and more frightful, I have never seen in the world?'

She speaks (thus): 'I am thy own bad actions (*kardār i bad*). I myself was ugly, and thou madest me worse day after day, and now thou hast thrown me and thine own self into misery and damnation, and we shall suffer punishment till the day of the Resurrection.'

And she embraces it, and both fall headlong from the middle of the Chinvat Bridge and descend to Hell.[25]

---

[24] SDBd. 99. 5–9 (ed. Dhabhar, p. 168–169). Quoted in the Rivāyat of Kāmā Bahrā, cf. RivDH., vol. I, p. 149–150.

[25] SDBd. 99. 15–20 (ed. Dhabhar, p. 169); see also RivDH. vol. I, p. 150.

ADDENDUM

ON THE FIGURES THAT MEET THE SOUL IN MANICHAEISM

As a special supplement here (see remarks in the Preface) it may be of interest to add a point or two to show in this connection the influence exercised by Zoroastrianism upon Manichaeism with regard to Mānī's doctrine of the figures that meet the soul immediately after death. Still more can be adduced later in respect to other direct parallels involved, such as the personages who act as judges and the weighing in the balance.[26] Our interest for the moment is in indicating how Mānī, a Persian by blood, employed elements from Zarathushtra's ancient faith when he sought to set up a new religion in the third century A.D., not only for Iran but for the world.

The sources which prove this influence are not merely accounts derived from outside but those recently discovered in actual Manichaean texts brought to light in Central Asia. All these are discussed in detail by my teacher, Professor Jackson, in the chapters of his forthcoming work on 'Mānī and Manichaeism,' which it has been my privilege to consult. From the material that he has made available I present here an outline of the most striking parallels in the Manichaean doctrine to the subjects treated in this chapter.

A well-known passage in an-Nadīm's Fihrist (A.D. 987, but based on older sources) is particularly pertinent. It tells, as in Zoroastrianism, of gods that greet the soul at once after death, but more especially mentions the significant figure of a Maiden. This passage, as translated from the Fihrist by Jackson, runs as follows, the Zoroastrian parallels being easily recognized:—

> Mānī says: 'When the death of one of the Righteous (Elect) occurs, Primal Man sends to him a God of Light

[26] See below, page 68, note 42; page 81, note 44.

in the form of the Wise Guide, accompanied by Three Gods²⁷ . . . With them comes also the M a i d e n, the s e m b l a n c e of the spirit of that righteous one.

There appears to him likewise the D e m o n of Greed and Lust, and (other) d e m o n s. As soon as he sees these he implores help from the Gods, (namely from) the one who is in the form of the Wise One and from the (other) three Gods. These then draw near to him; and when the d e m o n s see them they t u r n and flee.' ²⁸

In the case of the wicked, in similarity to the Zoroastrian doctrine, the Fihrist adds this:—

As regards the sinful man (i.e. the Wicked), whom Greed and Lust dominate, when his death takes place the D e m o n s c o m e to him, and they s e i z e and t o r m e n t him, and show him terrible things. [Ultimately they lead him to Hell.]²⁹

The likeness between the immediate fates experienced by the Pious and the Impious respectively makes clear the influence exercised upon the later so-called 'heresy' of Mānī by the older religion of Zarathushtra in regard to these vivid scenes.

Not only that. An actual Manichaean document from Turfan, preserved in old Turkish, has much to add regarding the 'grisly She-demon' who comes with other fiends to drag off the soul of the damned after it has been weighed at the Judgment. I add the rendering by Jackson (based on Le Coq) of this particular Turkish Manichaean Fragment (T. II. D. 178 verso, lines 1–12) because it recounts—

---

[27] Concerning the identification of these 'Gods' see Jackson, *JAOS.* 43. 20, and cf. below, page 68, note 42.

[28] Compare also Flügel, *Mani*, p. 69–70 (Arabic text) and p. 100 (transl.); likewise Kessler, *Mani*, p. 398–399 (transl.).

[29] Fihrist, see Flügel, p. 71 (text), p. 101 (transl.); cf. Kessler, p. 400 (transl.).

> The coming of the lying, hairy, grisly She-demon (and) her seizing of the wandering souls! Into the dark hell she drags (the soul) away, it is said. Smiting it upon the head she thrusts (it) down, it is said. . . . The demons in hell seize them, it is said. The ——— [?] ——— Demons come, it is said. The [??? obscure names in the text], it is said. To beg for death is useless![30]

Still another Turkish Manichaean Fragment, to be connected directly with the former, speaks not only of 'ten thousand cloud-black Demons' that come to afflict the lost soul, but it adds likewise a worse description of this grizzled demoness than that of the traditional hag in the Zoroastrian picture. According to the Turkish text (T. II. D. 169, iii, lines 16–22)—

> The lying, hairy, grisly She-demon comes, it is said. Her forehead [??] with its brows is like a cloud of hail, it is said; her glance is like a bloody dart [?], it is said. Her dug is like a dark-colored nail.[31]

And the text goes on to describe how a gray cloud issues from her nose and black smoke pours from her throat, while her breast is made up of a thousand snakes. The whole picture shows how Mānī's fertile imagination had caught up and elaborated an old idea in Zoroastrianism, just as it preserved, but did not elaborate, the vision of the Maiden referred to as the counterpart.

---

[30] See Le Coq, *Türkische Manichaica*, 2, p. 13, for text and German translation of this Fragment.

[31] See Le Coq, *op. cit.* p. 11.

CHAPTER VII

THE INDIVIDUAL JUDGMENT ACCORDING TO THE GĀTHĀS

Introduction. The soul now stands at the Individual Judgment [1] in the presence of one or more heavenly assessors before whom the life-account is rendered. The good and evil deeds are weighed in the balance; and the final decision is made according to the turn of the scales, which are counterpoised with perfect justice. Next comes the crossing of the Chinvat Bridge, the Bridge of Judgment, over which the righteous and the wicked alike must pass—the one to felicity, the other to damnation. This doctrine of an individual judgment at the Bridge is clearly discernible throughout the Zoroastrian scriptures, from the Gāthās to the latest Persian religious writings.[1a]

The store of Good Works, and their accounting. This doctrine of a spiritual accounting of man's life record, the weighing of merits and demerits, forms an integral part of Zarathushtra's message, as is shown by the Gāthās.

Zarathushtra devoutly questions Ahura Mazdāh:—

> These things I ask Thee, O Ahura, what verily is coming and is to come? What c l a i m s (*išudō*) in the e n t r i e s above (*dāθranąm*) shall be made upon the righteous, and what upon the wicked, O Mazdāh, (and) how shall these be when in the r e c k o n i n g (*hąnkərətā*)? [2]

---

[1] As in Roman Catholic theology, the Judgment is here called Individual or Particular to distinguish it from the Universal or General Judgment which takes place at the end of the world. The Zoroastrian doctrine of the General Judgment will be treated in a separate monograph to be published subsequently.

[1a] Parallels to the Bridge of Judgment can be cited in other religions as well, cf. G. A. F. Knight, art. 'Bridge' in *ERE*. 2. 852-854.

[2] Ys. 31. 14; cf. Jackson, *Hymn of Zoroaster*, p. 44-47, where the very full notes bring out clearly the real force and significance of the technical terms *išudō* and *dāθranąm*; *hąnkərətā* is a locative singular, 'in the reckoning.'

This Gāthic stanza brings out the characteristic marks of the doctrine. All the daily actions of man are entered, so to speak, as items (*dāθra*) of debit and credit in the record for the hereafter; and only by increasing the credit side of the account can the debits be counterbalanced.[3] When the account is brought to a final reckoning (*hənkərətā*), if there be any excess of good deeds, as in the case of the righteous, these souls find their final destiny in the Abode of Good Thought or House of Song.[4] But if, owing to bad deeds, the claims (*išudō*) cannot be satisfied, the result is reversed, as in the case of the wicked, who are destined to become veritable inmates of the House of the Lie.[5] In the third case, those whose wrong and right deeds exactly balance shall be consigned to a separate place.[6]

The same trend of thought as to the threefold destiny is to be noticed in the following Gāthic stanzas:—

> As he (i.e. Zarathushtra) shall act in accordance with those things which are the laws of the first life (i.e. the present life), so shall he as Judge [7] act with the most just deed concerning the wicked, and the righteous, and the one whose wrong and whose right deeds balance.[8]

Or again:—

> (The wicked) who with evil intent increase wrath and cruelty by their tongues—not being cattle-raisers among

[3] Cf. Jackson, *op. cit.* p. 45.
[4] Cf. Ys. 32. 15; 46. 10, 15-17; 50. 4; 51. 15.
[5] Cf. Ys. 49. 11; 46. 11; 31. 20; etc.
[6] Cf. Ys. 33. 1 (see below, n. 8), etc. An account of the threefold destiny of man (Heaven, Hell, and Hamistakān) is reserved for treatment elsewhere.
[7] The *ratav* is, no doubt, Zarathushtra himself, cf. Ys. 27. 13; 31. 2; see below, page 57.
[8] Ys. 33. 1. Bartholomae was the first to recognize in this stanza the later Zoroastrian doctrine of Hamistakān (in *ZDMG*. 35. 157-158). Roth's paper on the subject (two years later in *ZDMG*. 37. 223-229) is well known. The word *həmə-myāsaitē*, as a compound of *həm* = Skt. *sam*, and the root *myas-*, 'mix,' would mean 'commingle, mix in equal parts,' hence 'balance.' See Bthl. *AirWb.* 1190. Cf. also below, page 74, note 9.

ACCORDING TO THE GĀTHĀS 51

those that raise cattle [9]—whose good deeds do not surpass (i.e. outweigh) [10] their evil deeds, all these (will be) in the House [11] of the Daēvas (demons) [12] through the religion [13] of the Wicked One.[14]

All meritorious deeds are regarded as stored up in the treasure-house of Heaven, where they are entrusted to the divine protection of Mazdāh:—

And I will entrust, O Mazdāh, for keeping in Thy House,[15] this, (namely) the Good Thought and the souls of the Righteous, their homage and zeal, which is Devotion, that Thou mayest guard [16] them, O Mighty Ruler,[17] with enduring vigilance.[18]

Him (i.e. Ahura Mazdāh) shalt thou seek to win for us by hymns of homage, for now have I beheld with

---

[9] A Gāthic parenthesis. The wicked referred to are the followers of Bendva, the *daēvayasna* chieftain mentioned in the same Gāthā, stanzas 1 and 2. They were the greatest foes of the new religion of the Prophet.

[10] An example of the instr. neut. pl. as subject. The form *vqs* is 3d sg. aor. from *van-*, 'win, conquer.' See Jackson, *JAOS*. 15. Proc. p. lxii, and cf. Bthl. *AirWb*. 1350, as well as Bthl. in *BB*. 13. 82.

[11] *dqn*, loc. sg. of *dam-*, 'house.' See Bthl. *AirWb*. 684 and Bthl. in *GIrPh*. I. 224, § 402.

[12] A Gāthic designation for Hell; the word *daēvąng* is taken as gen. pl., after Bthl. *AirWb*. 667.

[13] Bartholomae renders *daēnā* here as 'Ego.' His version of this difficult line is somewhat different (see *AirWb*. 666 and *Gatha's des Awesta*, p. 95).

[14] Ys. 49. 4. The term Wicked One (*drəgvatō*) is a Gāthic appellation of Angra Mainyu, see Jackson, *GIrPh*. 2. 650 and n. 2, and also p. 651 mid.; cf. also Bthl. *AirWb*. 776. This stanza is closely parallel in thought to Ys. 51. 14.

[15] Read as *ā dqm*; loc. sg. of *dam-*, 'house.' The 'house' here referred to is the Depository, which is later known as *ganj*, 'treasury,' cf. p. 76–77, below. See Bthl. *AirWb*. 684, notes 2 and 3, and *AF*. 3. 49.

[16] Thus Bartholomae, dividing *avəmīrā* into *avəm īrā*, and taking the former as inf. 'to guard, for keeping.' See Bthl. *AirWb*. 179–180, 372; differently Scheftelowitz, *Asia Major*, 1. 487 n. 1.

[17] Read as one word: *mqzā.xšaθrā*.

[18] Ys. 49. 10.

mine eye this (Kingdom) of Good Thought, Deed, and Word, after having known Ahura Mazdāh through Asha (Righteousness); therefore let us lay down our prayers before Him in the House of Song.[19]

Or again:—

All the works of the Good Spirit with thought of Thee, the works of the holy man whose soul is in accord with Right, together with the hymns of praise in prayer to You, O Mazdāh, do Ye [20] deposit in the heavenly precinct.[21]

That it is Mazdāh who is the keeper of the true account can also be gathered from the following stanza:—

The many sins [22] by which he (i.e. Grehma) [23] has come to be known [24]—if so he be through these [25]— Thou knowest through Thy Best Thought, O Ahura, Thou who rememberest (man's) deserts.[26] In Thy Kingdom, O Mazdāh, shall Your pronouncement, and that of Asha, decide (i.e. be final).[27]

---

[19] Ys. 45. 8.

[20] That is, Mazdāh and the other Ahuras.

[21] Ys. 34. 2. The allusion is to the place where the meritorious actions are stored up for the future, called the Treasury in later times. See especially the remarks of Bthl. *AirWb.* 864 on *pairigaēθa*.

[22] The sins of defrauding mankind of happy life, as referred to in stanza 5 of the same chapter.

[23] Refers to Grehma, the powerful opponent of the Prophet, named in stanzas 12, 13, 14 of the same chapter and in Frahang i Oīm, chap. 21, see Reichelt, *WZKM.* 14. 205; 15. 136.

[24] The word ənāxštā is 3d sg. s-aor. mid.; cf. Skt. *naś-*, 'to attain, get'; Bthl. *AirWb.* 1056; *srāvahyeitī* is inf., cf. Bthl. *AirWb.* 1645.

[25] Another instance of Gāthic parenthesis. For similar instances in the Veda see Pischel and Geldner, *Vedische Studien*, 2. 91, 99, 229, 290.

[26] *hātā-marānay-*, 'mindful of one's merits'; cf. also Jackson in *JAOS.* 14. Proc. p. xx–xxi, and see Bthl. *AirWb.* 1802.

[27] Ys. 32. 6. The reference is to the Final Dispensation.

So far we have endeavored to show that the Gāthās contain a well-defined doctrine of the reckoning of man's merits and demerits and of a judgment on his life-record. There is no doubt that this takes place at the Individual Judgment, and before the twofold award is meted out to the souls, with a possible intermediate state.

The Judgment at the Chinvat Bridge. We are not in a position, however, to determine with precision the time when the Individual Judgment takes place. The Gāthās are completely silent on the point. It is a matter of little concern to the Prophet whether the Judgment takes place immediately after death or on the dawn of the fourth day after death. That the fate of each man is determined in strict accordance with the kind of life he has led on earth, or 'the first life,' [28] is the thing that is of moment. If one may be allowed to express an opinion on this problem, the writer is inclined to believe, in the absence of any evidence to the contrary, that the Gāthās point to a judgment which takes place immediately at the conclusion of 'the first life,' rather than to one at the dawn of the fourth day after death, as described in the Later Avesta and in the Pahlavi writings.

Another important observation to be made in this connection is that Zarathushtra's teaching [29] of a strict reckoning of man's actions leaves no room for a real remission of sins, whereas later Zoroastrianism admits repentance, expiation, and remission. 'The laws of the first life' [30] cannot be turned aside or altered by any sacrifice or offering; and it is in accordance with these laws that man shall be judged, both here and hereafter.[31] Yet, in

[28] The life of man, according to the Gāthās, falls into two parts: its earthly portion and that which is lived after death. Cf. Geldner, art. 'Zoroaster' in *Enc. Brit.* (11th ed.) 28. 1039–1043, especially p. 1042.

[29] Geldner rightly observes that no religion has grasped the ideas of guilt and merit so clearly as they are depicted in the Gāthās of Zoroaster. Cf. Geldner, *op. cit.* p. 1042.

[30] Ys. 33. 1.

[31] This tenet of a strict reckoning and balancing of man's actions coincides remarkably with the principle of Persian jurisprudence, whereby an accused man was judged on the whole record of his wrong-doings and his services.

54 THE INDIVIDUAL JUDGMENT

spite of this, we may infer that Zarathushtra's sense of justice allowed that strenuous effort in performing good deeds would ultimately create a surplus of merit to outweigh the accumulation of past evil.

The reckoning itself, the *judicium particulare*, is evidently comprehended under the word *ākā* [32] in the Gāthās; and the two stanzas given below clearly bring out this idea:—

> . . Those who live rightly according to Asha, among the many that see the sun, I [33] shall place in the Abodes of the Wise, when they stand in judgment.[34]
> . . . Will Thy Judgment (*ākā̊*), O Asha, be wished for by the pious [35]—the weighing [36] of the deeds of Good Thought? [37]

Closely associated with these is another Gāthic stanza, which may be worth quoting in full:—

> With praise will I worship You, O Mazdāh Ahura, together with Asha and Vahishta Manah and Khshathra, who will stand [38] by the faithful one [39] on the Path

---

Only if it was found that the former preponderated, could the extreme penalty be meted out. Herodotus bears evidence to this practice. See Hdt. 1. 137, and cf. Jackson, in *Actes du Xme Congr. Internat. Oriental., Session de Genève, 1894*, part 2, p. 71, 72 (Leiden, 1895).

[32] *ā-kā-* f. 'revelation, manifestation, judgment'; see Bthl. *AirWb.* 309, and cf. Geldner, *op. cit.* p. 1042.

[33] Mazdāh speaks in answer to Zarathushtra's questioning regarding the reward of the pious husbandman; cf. also Ys. 51. 5.

[34] Ys. 50. 2 c, d. *ākāstə̄ng* (*ākā-stā-* adj.), 'standing in (or before) the judgment.' Cf. Bthl. *AirWb.* 309.

[35] *arədrə̄ng išyā*, 'wished for by the pious'; cf. Ys. 50. 4, cited below.

[36] *javara-* m., 'weighing.' Bthl. *AirWb.* 605. A difficult word, whose meaning is doubtful.

[37] Ys. 48. 8 c, d. Here *vaŋhə̄uš manyə̄uš* is equivalent to Vohu Manah, as can be shown from Ys. 45. 5, 8; 34. 2.

[38] *stā̊ŋhat̲*, 3d pl.

[39] *sərāošānē*, lit. 'hearer, obedient.'

(*ā.paiθī*) of Judgment (*ākā̊*), wished for by the pious,[40] in the House of Song.[41]

We now turn to the important question as to the place where the Individual Judgment is held. There are many passages in the Gāthās which either expressly or by mere suggestion point to the well-known Chinvat Bridge as the scene of reckoning and balancing where the souls of both the pious and the wicked will stand in judgment. A very significant stanza connects the highly technical word *ākā*, noted above, with this *činvatō pərətav-*,[42] the 'Bridge of the Separator,' where the souls of the wicked are depicted as suffering grievous pain:—

> Therefore the Daēnā of the wicked destroys the verity of the Right Way for him, and his soul shall suffer anguish [43] at the Judgment (*ākā̊*) of the Chinvat Bridge, having strayed from the Path of Asha through his own deeds and tongue.[44]

It is at the Bridge, moreover, that the first separation [45] of the pious from the wicked shall take place—the separation which is mentioned in the following Gāthic stanza:—

[40] *išō . . . arədrǝ̄ng*, cf. above *arədrǝ̄ng išyā* in Ys. 48. 8 c. *išō* is gen. sg. in apposition with *ākā̊*; lit. 'the judgment (which is) the desire of the pious.' Differently Bthl. *AirWb*. 309.

[41] Ys. 50. 4.

[42] *činvant-*, pres. participle (from ¹ *kay-* vb.), 'separating,' only in the gen. sg., *činvatō* with *pərətav-*, 'Bridge of the Separator.' In LAv. it occurs also as *činvat̰.pərətav-* f.; in Phl. vers. as *činvat* (transcrip. *č d n n d*) *pūhl*; also as *čandōr.puhl* in Pāzend; in the Skt. vers. either as *cinuadanāma-setuḥ* (e.g. on Ys. 51. 13) or as *candorapuhalanāmā setuḥ* (e.g. MX. 2. 115, 162). See Bthl. *AirWb*. 596, 597.

[43] *xraodaitī* (3d sg. subjunctive act., here intrans.), 'be in torment.' Cf. Bthl. *AirWb*. 533.

[44] Ys. 51. 13; see also above, page 31.

[45] This is purposely called the first separation (*činvant-*) to distinguish it from the second, the division which will take place at the time of the General Judgment. The latter is technically known in the Gāthās as the *vī-dātay-* 'division' (like the Biblical 'separation of the sheep from the goats'). Note the passages on the subject in Bthl. *AirWb*. 1443.

Therefore the Karpans and the Kavis [46] perish [47]
through those (very ones) whom they do not allow to
rule over their life at will. These (i.e. the faithful)
shall be carried away from them both to the
Abode of Good Thought.[48]

The Judges at the assize. This leads to an extremely difficult
problem as to who is the Judge at this *judicium particulare*
and who is the Separator. There are numerous passages in the
Gāthās where Ahura Mazdāh is invoked by Zarathushtra as
the Ruler (*xšayąs*) over the twofold awards,[49] who at the time
of the Final Dispensation will divide the wise from the unwise.[50]
He is the supreme arbiter, and His decision is final.[51] At the
time of the Resurrection it is Zarathushtra, so we gather from
the Gāthās, who will be the *ratav* (Judge), Mazdāh being the
ahū (Overlord); and Zarathushtra expressly declares himself to
be the *ratav* appointed by Ahura.[52] After a thorough study of
this crucial question, the author is inclined to believe that the
figure of the Separator at the Bridge is that of Ahura Mazdāh,
assisted, no doubt, by his fellow-Ahuras (the Amesha Spentas),[53]
the supreme function being one and the same at this particular

---

[46] Literally, 'that which is karpandom and kavidom,' referring to the two
daēva-worshiping communities, who were opposed to the religion of the Prophet.
For the secondary suffix *-tāt* forming f. abs. (or, as here, collective) nouns,
see Jackson, *Av. Grammar*, § 842; also Reichelt, *Aw. Elementarbuch*, § 358;
cf. Bthl. *AirWb.* 455, 466.

[47] More exactly, 'hath [already] come to destruction' (*vī.nə̄nāsā*, Bthl.
AirWb. 1056). The future is regarded as having been already accomplished.

[48] Ys. 32. 15. The abode of heavenly bliss as opposed to the Abode of the
Worst Thought, mentioned in stanza 13.

[49] Ys. 51. 5 etc.

[50] Ys. 31. 19; 47. 6 (*vīdātay-*).

[51] Ys. 51. 14; 32. 6.

[52] See especially Ys. 33. 1 (cf. above, p. 50), 31. 2; and cf. Bthl. *AirWb.*
s.v. *ahū-*, 281–282, and *ratav-*, 1498–1502; cf. also Ys. 51. 5; 44. 16. As
Moulton has rightly pointed out (*EZ.* p. 168), there is nothing in the least
incongruous or self-assertive in the Prophet's claim, nor does it seriously
militate against his authorship.

[53] Cf. Ys. 50. 4, cited above, and Ys. 51. 14.

ACCORDING TO THE GĀTHĀS

judgment as at the universal. It seems probable, furthermore, that the *ratav* who will judge men on their life-record is Zarathushtra, who will act as Judge both at the Individual and at the General Judgment.

A Gāthic stanza, which may, however, refer to the General Judgment, expressly mentions Mazdāh as the one

> who will separate [54] the wise from the unwise through
> His knowing counselor, Asha.[55]

Another Gāthic passage, cited above [56] in connection with the balancing of men's deeds, needs to be considered at this juncture. If we are correct in interpreting its import, Zarathushtra is here described as one who takes command of this existence and 'shall act in accordance with those things which are the laws of the present life'; in other words, as he shall act as Overlord (*ahū*) in this world,[57] though the term is not expressly mentioned,

> so shall he act as Judge (*ratav*) with the most just deed concerning the wicked, and the righteous, and the one whose wrong and right deeds balance.[56]

One further point to be noted in the foregoing passage is the epithet *razišta* ('most just'), which is particularly applied to the abstraction of Justice, Rashnu, in the later scriptural writings, in which he assumes great importance as one of the three judges at the Chinvat Bridge, where he holds the balance in which are weighed men's merits and demerits.[58] Closely associated with Rashnu in other parts of the Avesta, as well as in the Pahlavi literature, are Mithra and Sraosha; but in the Gāthās the term *miθra* occurs only once, being used in the sense of 'ties of faith'

[54] *vīčinaot* (¹ *kay-* vb., with *vī*), 'will separate, distinguish.' Cf. Bthl. *AirWb.* 441.
[55] Ys. 46. 17 c, d; cf. above, pages 52, 54.
[56] Ys. 33. 1, see above, page 50.
[57] Cf. the Ahuna Vairya formula (Ys. 27. 13), where Zarathushtra is declared to be both *ahū* and *ratav*, the lord of men's conduct in the first life, and the judge of their actions in the life hereafter.
[58] See Bthl. *AirWb.* 1515; also Jackson, *GIrPh.* 2. 642.

or 'compact.'[59] Hence we must maintain a certain attitude of reserve, so far as the Gāthās are concerned, with regard to this well known Indo-Iranian divinity. Sraosha is a truly Gāthic figure, appearing a number of times in the Gāthās, twice in connection with the General Judgment.[60]

From these general observations concerning what later becomes the triad of judges, let us turn once more to Zarathushtra's more precise promises and warnings for the individual when he shall stand in judgment at the Chinvat Bridge. The Prophet will act not only as the Judge at the Bridge, but also as the guide [61] for those who have followed the path of Asha in accordance with his teachings:—

> Whoso, man or woman, O Mazdāh Ahura, shall give unto me that which Thou knowest as the best for life, [grant Thou unto them] the Kingdom through Vohu Manah as the reward for Righteousness. And with all those whom I will urge to invoke You will I c r o s s over the Chinvat Bridge.[62]

On the other hand, the wicked, who have rejected the revelation of the Prophet, shall be utterly confounded when they come to the Bridge of the Separator:—

[59] Ys. 46. 5; see Bthl. *AirWb.* 1183, and Moulton, *EZ.* p. 67.
[60] Ys. 33. 5; 43. 12; cf. Bthl. *AirWb.* 1634.
[61] Moulton (*EZ.* p. 166) seems to take the first line of Ys. 46. 17, where Zarathushtra declares that he will plead for his followers as their advocate before Mazdāh, as referring to the Individual Judgment. The present writer, however, believes that the scene is laid at the Consummation, mentioned in stanza 14. The same criticism can be applied to Ys. 34. 1, where Zarathushtra promises that he 'will give Immortality and Right and the Kingdom of Welfare' in Mazdāh's name (*EZ.* p. 167, 168), and likewise to the case of Ys. 43. 12 (*EZ.* p. 169), as well as to the 'pointing of the hand,' which is that of Mazdāh, at the separation of 'faithful' and 'hostile,' as in Ys. 34. 4 and 43. 4 (*EZ.* p. 169). It must, in all fairness, be admitted that it is a very difficult problem to distinguish definitely and clearly the picture of a particular judgment from the supreme spectacle of a universal judgment, as contained in the Gāthās.
[62] Ys. 46. 10.

ACCORDING TO THE GĀTHĀS

Through their power the Karpans and the Kavis have yoked [63] man up with evil deeds in order to destroy his (future) life, but their own soul and their own Daēnā will cause them anguish [64] when they come where the Chinvat Bridge is, to be dwellers in the House of the Druj for all eternity.[65]

Conclusion. To summarize this chapter, we have seen that the Gāthās contain the doctrine of a strict reckoning of man's actions, and that this doctrine is described in no uncertain terms —Zarathushtra's promises and warnings are direct and precise. We can also gather from the Gāthās that the reckoning and balancing of the merits and the demerits takes place at the Chinvat Bridge, and we can likewise say with certainty that Zarathushtra, inspired by Mazdāh to know the truth and the Right Way, will be the one to judge mankind there, whereas Mazdāh, the supreme arbiter, shall separate the righteous from the wicked for future beatitude or torment. In short, we have tried to show that the Gāthās contain, at least in substance, those essential elements that are elaborated in the Later Avesta and in the Pahlavi books. We can say without hesitation that the doctrine of the Individual Judgment [66] is one of the cardinal teachings of Zarathushtra concerning the life hereafter, even though we possess only the outline touches which the brush of the master artist, bold and firm, has traced, leaving the canvas to be filled in by the hand of lesser painters whom his imagination had inspired.

[63] See above, page 31, note 20.

[64] *xraodaṯ*, 3d sg. subjunctive act., used transitively, from the verb *xraod-*; cf. Bthl. *AirWb.* 533

[65] Ys. 46. 11.

[66] Söderblom seems to doubt the appearance of this doctrine as early as the Gāthās. See *Rev. de l'histoire des religions*, 40. 266–276, where he reviews Stave's book on the influence of Parsism on Judaism, and note especially p. 274. See Moulton's comment in *EZ.* p. 169, 170.

CHAPTER VIII

THE INDIVIDUAL JUDGMENT ACCORDING TO THE LATER AVESTA

Introduction. In the previous chapter we tried to bring out from the Gāthās the salient features of what becomes in the later writings an established dogma of Zoroastrianism. The present chapter will elaborate upon these as contained in the Later Avesta. We find in these younger portions of the sacred texts many allusions to the account kept by Mazdāh or by one or another of his ministering angels, and to the store of good works laid up in heaven. There is also the Chinvat Bridge, to which both the pious and the wicked must go. There are many references likewise to the tribunal of justice and the balancing of man's good and bad actions, besides other details. All these we shall take up in a sequence parallel to that already used.

The store of Good Works recorded. That an account was kept by Mazdāh may be gathered from the Yasht devoted to his praise and worship, where the sixteenth of the several names attributed to him is *hāta.marənay-*, 'remembering man's deserts,' as the recorder of true reckoning.[1]

Or, again, it is Asha Vahishta, or Best Righteousness, personified in the Fire, who is the keeper of a record, a special reference to this being found in a metrical passage in the Yasna:—

> Every righteous man that cometh making his absolution with this in a benediction, mayest thou (Asha) c r e d i t (*paiti.barāhi*) with good thoughts, good words, good deeds.[2]

[1] Yt. 1. 8; cf. Ys. 32. 6, see above, page 52, n. 26; see also Bthl. *AirWb.* 1802. These are the only two instances where the word occurs.

[2] Ys. 55. 4; cf. Jackson, *JAOS.* 13, Proc. (Oct. 1887), p. ccviii, ccxii. Bartholomae renders it differently: 'receive him in *Humata, Hūxta* and *Hvaršta*,' i.e. in the three antechambers of Paradise; cf. *AirWb.* 1851.

This doctrine thus inculcated of 'laying up treasures in heaven' occurs also in the Yasht dedicated to Mithra:—

> Hearken unto our prayer, O Mithra, let our prayer be acceptable to thee, O Mithra, fulfil thou[3] our prayer; come to our libations, come to them when offered, put these to our account (*čimāne*),[4] lay them down (*nī . . . dasva*) in the House of Song.[5]

The Hadhōkht Nask appears to contain still another allusion to the store of good works. In the interim after the soul of the righteous sees its own Daēnā, and before it passes through the three stages that lead to Heaven, Ahura Mazdāh lays, as it were, before this pious one the fruits of his former good actions:—

> [Ahura speaks:] These (are thy) good thoughts, these (are thy) good words, these (are thy) good deeds. Then hereafter men will worship me, (who am) Ahura Mazdāh, the long-worshiped One (*darəγō.yaštəmča*) and the One whose counsel is sought (*həm.parštəmča*).[6]

We observed above that in the spiritual life the records of all actions, good and bad, are entered as items, and that the debit can be balanced only by adding to the credit side, no item being erased. A notable passage in the Visprat brings out this idea very definitely:—

> Hold feet, hands, mind ready, O ye worshipers of Mazdāh and followers of Zarathushtra, for doing lawful,

---

[3] *upa . . . āhiša* ([1] *āh-*), opt. mid. 2d sg. with *i*, instead of *ī*; cf. Bthl. *AirWb.* 345.

[4] Differently Bthl. *AirWb.* 597, 'for atoning.'

[5] Yt. 10. 32.

[6] HN. 2. 14b; so also Geldner, *Religionsgeschichtliches Lesebuch*, p. 353 and n. 1, 2), to whom belongs the credit for this new interpretation; the other translators seem to regard these words as the concluding part of the Maiden's speech, cf. likewise Bthl. *AirWb.* 695, 1809.

well-ordered, good deeds; but hold back from doing unlawful, ill-ordered deeds; and practise ye in this world (*iδa*) the good deeds of husbandry, in order to pay off (*daste*) [7] with a surplus (*anuyamnāiš*) your deficits (*uyamna*).[8]

The Judgment as described in the Vidēvdāt. These items (*dāθra*) which a man puts down to the account of his soul are brought to a final reckoning, and the entries are balanced at the Judgment of the Chinvat Bridge. This idea, together with other details, can be gathered from the following account given in the Vidēvdāt (19. 27-30):—

(27) [Zarathushtra asked Ahura Mazdāh:] 'O Creator of the material world, Thou Holy One! Where are the entries (*dāθra*) recorded,[9] where are the entries compared (with one another),[10] where are the entries brought to completion, where are the entries balanced,[11] (which) a man in the material world puts down for (i.e. to the account of) his own soul?'

(28) Then spake Ahura Mazdāh: 'After a man has passed away, after a man has come to his end, after the wicked evil-minded Demons cut the thread,[12] on

---

[7] *daste*, verbal abstract, infin. from *dā*-, 'give, pay.'

[8] Vr. 15. 1. The word *uyamna* is a pres. ptcpl. from the passive of [3] *vā*-, and would mean lit. 'what is found wanting,' hence 'deficit.' Cf. Jackson, *JAOS.* 14, Proc. (Oct. 1888), p. xx–xxi; see also Bthl. *AirWb.* 1407, 701–702.

[9] *bavainti*, 'become, take place, come into existence,' hence 'are recorded.'

[10] Reading as +*pairyeinte*, 'are compared,' following Bthl. *AirWb.* 733 (s.v. *dāθra*-), 849 (s.v. [1] *par*-). In the latter citation he gives the singular, +*pairyete*.

[11] *paiti.hənjasənte*, 'come together over against each other,' the balancing of the credit side as against the debit. All the terms employed here or elsewhere in the accounting are doubtless taken from the daily language of the people as used in their commercial transactions.

[12] The words *pairiθnəm dərəninti* present some difficulty. Bthl., *AirWb.* 865, 742, does not render them, saying that the reading is uncertain. Darmesteter interprets them as 'cut off his eyesight.' The present writer

ACCORDING TO THE LATER AVESTA 63

the third night [13] the dawn [14] begins to brighten,[15] the morning light [16] begins to shine forth, Mithra,[17] the well-armed, ascends [18] the mountains that possess felicity through Asha [19]; the sun is rising.[20]

(29) The Demon Vīzaresha [21] by name, O Spitama Zarathushtra, leads away in bonds [22] the soul of the

takes *pairiθna-* as 'thread,' derived from the root *tan-*, 'stretch,' and regards *dərəninti*, 'they cut,' as from ¹ *dar-*, 'cut'; see also Geldner, *Sitzungsberichte der Preuss. Akad. Wiss.* (Berlin, 1903), p. 425 n. 2. Cf. Vd. 18. 19, 21; and for a similar idea see Yt. 8. 54. Dr. Haas calls my attention to the Biblical parallel in the 'silver cord' of Ecclesiastes 12. 6.

[13] *θritya̅ xšapō* is a genitive of time. See Reichelt, *Aw. Elementarbuch*, § 507.

[14] A problematic word. *uši°* in the loc. sg. occurs elsewhere as the first part of a compound; here it appears to be used independently as a nom. sg. with transfer of declension from *ušah-*: *uš-* f. 'dawn'; cf. Skt. *uṣas* and Phl. vers. *uš* [Pāzand *ōš* or *hōš*]; compare (but differently) Bthl. *AirWb.* 415. Geldner's text is here followed in retaining the form *uši* on the authority of many good mss.; Bartholomae prefers to take the form *usi-raočaiti*, following the mss. L4 and B2, see *AirWb.* 1487, s.v. *raok-*.

[15] *vīusaiti* (¹ *vah-*); cf. Skt. *ucchati*; the Phl. vers. has *vičāšišnīh*.

[16] *bāmyā-* f., lit. 'the light (goddess),' i.e. Dawn. Cf. the Phl. transcrip. *bāmīk*; see Bthl. *AirWb.* 955. Note that the two separate words for dawn in the Avesta, *ušah-* and *bāmyā-*, are often combined into one word in Pahlavi and Pāzand writings: *ušbāmīk, hōšbām*. A well-known prayer in the Khvartak Apastāk, composed of selections from the Ys., Vd., and other parts of the Avesta, is entitled *Hōšbām*.

[17] Acc. sg. instead of nom. sg. Mithra is clearly connected with the sun, but not yet identical with it, as he became in later times.

[18] *āsnaoiti* (² *had-*); cf. Bthl. *AirWb.* 1755.

[19] The mountains of Holy Felicity are meant, doubtless with a reference to the *Harā Bərəzaitī*, mentioned in § 30; cf. also Yt. 10. 13, 50.

[20] Cf. on this verse Lommel in *Zeit. f. Indologie u. Iranistik*, 3. 177–178; and also Geldner, *Religionsgeschichtliches Lesebuch*, p. 354.

[21] *Vīzarəša*, lit. 'who drags away,' is the demon who binds the soul of the wicked and drags it off to the Chinvat Bridge, as noted in this paragraph, and then to Hell after Judgment, as described in the next paragraph. See above, pages 24, 38; cf. Bthl. *AirWb.* 1471.

[22] Note the PhlVd. comm.: 'He casts (*ōftēt*) a noose (*band*) round the neck of every man when he dies. If righteous, the noose falls from his neck; if wicked, he is dragged with that noose down into Hell.' A similar idea may be noted in the Mahābhārata, which refers to the noose (*pāśa*) of Yama, the god of death, cf. E. W. Hopkins, *Epic Mythology*, p. 112–113, Strassburg, 1915.

64 THE INDIVIDUAL JUDGMENT

wicked, the lost-life [23] of the Demon-worshiping men, (when) [24] he comes to the Paths [25] made by Zrvan,[26] that for the wicked and that for the righteous,—to the Chinvat Bridge created by Mazdāh, (and) [24] they (i.e. the Judges) demand of the consciousness [27] and soul that share of worldly goods given in the material world.[28]

(30a) She (namely, the Maiden), beautifully formed, strong, fair-faced, comes (to the Chinvat Bridge),[29] with

[23] *marazujītīm*, 'lost-life.' Doubtful. Bthl. (*AirWb*. 1174) does not offer any definite suggestion as to the meaning of the word. Darmesteter translates it by 'qui vivent dans le péché' and says that the rendering is conjectural. See his *ZA*. 2. 269, 268 n. 64.

[24] There is an asyndeton in the concise expression of the text itself, lit. 'he comes . . . they demand' etc., which has been filled out to make the sense clearer.

[25] Bartholomae (*AirWb*. 847) rightly regards the phrase as expressing an objective or goal (for similar genitives of goal see Reichelt, *Aw. Elementarbuch*, § 497 end; note also *gairinąm ašax^vāθranąm* in Vd. 19. 28). Geldner, *Religionsgesch. Lesebuch*, p. 354, recognizes this in part by 'sie geht . . . die Wege.' In any case the sense is clear. We might expect here a dual form instead of the plural, for there are only two paths, one (*yasča*) for the wicked and the other (*yasča*) for the righteous (cf. also Yt. 4. 4), but perhaps the phrase was appropriately chosen as a generalized plural to include all the instances of the wicked and the righteous at the Judgment.

[26] *Zrvō.dātanąm*. It would scarcely be correct to claim, because of *Zrvō°*, that this sentence is a late interpolation in the text. The Zarvanic doctrine can be shown to go back at least to the fourth century preceding the Christian era, for Eudemus of Rhodes (about 300 B.C.), cited by Damascius (*Dubitationes et Solutiones*, 125bis), evidently refers to Zrvan under the name Chronos, 'Time' (cf. Clemen, *Nachrichten*, p. 131–132, 196, and *Fontes Hist. Relig. Pers.* p. 95).

[27] *baoδah-* is one of the spiritual faculties of man; see the note above, p. 33. This technical term has been variously interpreted, for which see Bthl. *AirWb*. 919. The nearest English word which can bring out the meaning of this Avestan word is 'consciousness' or 'perception,' preferably the former; cf. Jackson, *JAOS*. 13, Proc. (Oct. 1887), p. ccviii, ccxiv, and *Av. Reader*, p. 38; the Phl. vers. has *bōδ*, glossed elsewhere (Ys. 26) by *āšnāk*.

[28] The soul (here of the wicked) is questioned about the use made of its worldly goods, in order to ascertain its liberality, cf. Vd. 18. 34; 3. 34, 35.

[29] Note the same word *jasaiti* used here as above in § 29. In order to complete the picture we might repeat the words 'to the Paths . . . the material

the dogs at her side, wearing a bodice [30] and a crown,[30] dextrous and skilful.

(30b) He [31] (namely Vīzaresha) drags down (*nizaršaite*) the sinful [32] souls of the wicked to Darkness.[33]

world.' In the case of the wicked, it is *Vīzarəša* who drags them to the Seat of Judgment, whereas in that of the righteous it is the *Daēnā* who leads them before the heavenly tribunal.

[30] See the notes on these words (*nivavaiti* and *pusavaiti*) above, page 36.

[31] *hā*, thus all good mss., nom. sg. masc.; cf. Jackson, *Av. Grammar*, § 411; *hā* can also be a fem., but it is doubtful whether it here refers to the Maiden. If such a claim should be made, it may be suggested that it may allude to the goddess *Ārmatay*, who, according to Vd. 3. 35, throws down into the gloom of Hell the sinful man who does not deal justly with the good agriculturist. It would seem, however, that *hā* here refers to *Vīzarəša*. Note the radical *zarəš-* in the verb *nizaršaite*, which is the same root as that which is found in the name of the demon *Vīzarəša*.

[32] *ayəm*, ungrammatical, but the mss. show no variant. Perhaps a corrupt marginal note has crept into the text. Bthl. *AirWb*. 47 emends it to *ayąm*.

[33] The entire sentence is not translated in the Pahlavi version, and Geldner seems to regard it as an interpolation, enclosing it in square brackets. Wolff evidently follows Geldner's text in indicating it as an interpolation (see his *Avesta*, p. 431), as do Reichelt (*Av. Reader*, p. 65, 160) and Darmesteter (*ZA*. 2. 270); but Darmesteter omits it completely in his English translation (*SBE*. 4. 219). The present writer, however, does not believe that the clause is interpolated, and advances the following reasons in support of his argument. First, the clause is to be found in all the good manuscripts; secondly, the general sense of the subject described in § 27–32 would call for such a sentence in the text itself. In § 29 we are told that the demon Vīzaresha drags the soul of the wicked to the Judgment Seat, and that it is judged on its past record, but we are not told anything about its fate. The first part of § 30 matches exactly with § 29. It is concerned with the soul of the righteous, which seems to be brought to the Seat of Judgment by the beautiful Maiden. As in the case of the wicked, the soul of the righteous is also judged on its past record; but, though that is not explicitly mentioned in the text, we are entitled to fill in the gap from the preceding paragraph (§ 29). The judgment being thus rendered respectively to the wicked soul (§ 29) and to the righteous soul (§ 30a), what follows in § 30 (designated here as § 30b and § 30c) describes their final destiny. That of the former is depicted in § 30b, when it is dragged to Hell by the demon Vīzaresha, whereas that of the latter is described in § 30c, when it is made to cross the Chinvat Bridge and is led to Heaven by the Maiden. Thirdly, the writer believes that here we have a case in which the omission of the clause in the Pahlavi version is to be regarded as an oversight on the part of the copyists. The same word *hā* at the beginning of the

(30c) She (namely the Maiden) leads (*āsnaoiti*) the souls of the righteous across the lofty Harā, she supports (*vīδārayeiti*) them across the Chinvat Bridge on that span [34] to the spiritual Yazatas (angels).' [35]

These passages of the Vidēvdāt present a detailed picture not only of the events preceding the Individual Judgment, but also of those that immediately follow. We are thus told that the entries are reckoned up and balanced at the *judicium particulare* on the dawn of the fourth day after death (cf. § 27, 28); and we can further gather that this Judgment takes place at the Chinvat Bridge (cf. § 29), while its association with the lofty Harā (Alburz) is very significant (cf. § 30c). Equally pointed is the mention of Mithra, the god of light and truth, who goes up to the mountains, referring undoubtedly to the Harā range, and who presides at the heavenly tribunal (cf. § 29).

Next we are told how the souls of the wicked are dragged to the place of Judgment by the demon Vīzaresha, and the Judges, Mithra undoubtedly being one of them, give their verdict of condemnation (cf. § 29). Contrasted with this is the description of the Maiden who leads the souls of the righteous to the Seat of Judgment, where the formal pronouncement of the award of bliss is made (cf. § 30a). It is thus clear that when the Judgment has been rendered, the souls of the wicked are dragged to Hell by Vīzaresha (cf. § 30b), whereas those of the righteous are helped across the Chinvat Bridge and led to Heaven by the Maiden (cf. § 30c).

These central ideas can be supplemented from other texts

sentences (§ 30a, 30b) caused the copyists to skip a line (Geldner himself allows such instances of omission elsewhere in the Phl. vers., e.g. at Vd. 3. 27; see also the *Prolegomena* to his edition of the Avesta, p. 49). These considerations, noted above, give ground for belief in the genuineness of the text if explained as suggested, so that the sentence need not be regarded as an interpolation.

[34] Literally, 'on the bridgeway of the spiritual Yazatas'; see above, p. 36, n. 25.
[35] Vd. 19. 27–30.

of the Avesta. We shall first take up the question of the Judges who preside at the special judgment directly after death, before turning to the accounts concerning the Chinvat Bridge itself.

The triad of heavenly Judges. We noted above that Mithra is a judge at the Chinvat Bridge, yet he is not alone, for he is assisted in his work by two heavenly assessors, namely, Sraosha and Rashnu.[36] It would be well to observe that among this triad of judges Mithra is the most important. This old Indo-Iranian divinity reappears in the Later Avestan pantheon as the chief among the Yazatas. He is the embodiment of the sun's light, the angel of Truth—the pre-eminent Zoroastrian virtue—and as such the stern punisher of the sinner who breaks his word and pledge. As might be expected, the hymn of praise dedicated to Mithra (Yt. 10) is the most important of all the Yashts, and one of the longest. Mithra's close association with Sraosha and Rashnu can be shown from numerous Avestan passages.[37]

We are already familiar with the great role Sraosha plays not only during the lifetime of a person but also after his death. Though he is not specifically mentioned in the Later Avesta as a Judge at the Chinvat Bridge, his intimate association with Mithra and Rashnu is sufficient to reveal his own office at the Judgment.[38] In the well-known hymn dedicated to Sraosha (Ys. 57), we are told that he was the first to worship Ahura Mazdāh and the Amesha Spentas, as well as the first to worship

> both the Overseer and the Judge (*pāyū θwōrəštāra*) who pass Judgment upon all creatures.[39]

[36] Cf. the triad of Greek gods, Minos, Aeacus, and Rhadamanthys. Tiele's suggestion (*Religionsgesch.* p. 210) regarding the possible Greek influence on the Iranian triad of judges is questionable; see also Moulton, *EZ.* p. 167 n. 1.

[37] Cf. Yt. 10. 41, 100; 17. 16; Vr. 11. 6; Ys. 65. 12; 70. 3; see Bthl, *AirWb.* 1185, 1634, 1516; cf. also Jackson, *GIrPh.* 2. 642, 643.

[38] This we shall see in the next chapter on the Judgment in the Pahlavi literature, where the three are specifically mentioned as Judges at the Chinvat Bridge.

[39] Ys. 57. 2. Lit. 'both the keeper and the discriminator (copulative dual) who discriminate (or divide),' from the root *θwars-*, 'to cut, divide.' (Dif-

The writer believes that the 'Overseer' is Mithra and the 'Judge' is Rashnu.[40] They distinguish the good from the bad at the Chinvat Bridge, to which the evil as well as the just must come. In the light of this interpretation the invocation by Sraosha of his two co-assessors at the Judgment becomes very significant; and other allusions to Srōsh in the Pahlavi texts and elsewhere, as cited below,[41] tend to bear this out.[42]

As already noted, closely associated with Mithra and Sraosha is the divinity Rashnu. He is pre-eminently the angel of Justice, as his very epithet *razišta* indicates. In the Yasht dedicated to his praise and adoration (Yt. 12), Rashnu is invoked to come and attend the performance of the *var nīrang*, or ordeal, of which, as the Lord of Justice, he was the natural arbiter.[43] This primary function of Rashnu is quite in keeping with his office as one of the Judges at the Chinvat Bridge.

ferently Bthl., *AirWb.* 888, under *pāyav-*). There are two Yashts dedicated to Sraosha: besides this hymn (Ys. 57), known as the Srōsh Yasht, there is another but shorter one, known as the Srōsh Yasht Hadhōkht (Yt. 11).

[40] Bthl., *AirWb.* 889, seems to understand the two to be Mithra and Ahura; cf. the Phl. vers., which directly mentions Mithra. See Jackson, *Hymn of Zoroaster*, p. 26.

[41] See below, pages 82–83.

[42] In *JAOS.* 43. 20 ('postscript') Jackson, when dealing with probable influences of Zoroastrianism upon Manichaeism, refers to the Manichaean doctrine of 'three gods' who are especially concerned with the fate of the soul at the Judgment. He there alludes to the present writer's suggestion to make *Srōš* (together with the well-known Manichaean personifications *Xrōštag* and *Padvaxtag*) a member of the group which, while differing somewhat, would be parallel in general to the Zoroastrian idea of Mithra, Sraosha, and Rashnu. He has since called the writer's attention to a reference in the Chinese Manichaean Treatise (*JA*. 1911, p. 523) where *Srōš* is called the 'King who judges all matters.' It seems possible that Rashnu is referred to in this Chinese text (*op. cit.* p. 584) as the 'King of Justice.' In the Mandaean Liturgies the assessor who holds the scales at the tribunal (corresponding to Rashnu) is called *Abathur* (see Lidzbarski, *Mand. Liturgien*, p. 278 for references); and a somewhat late Mandaean text cited by W. Brandt (*Die mandäische Religion*, Leipzig, 1889, p. 195) expressly says that *Abatur* is 'Rashna and Rast in this world.' The pertinacity of such a phrase as the 'King who judges all matters' would point to the ancient office of Sraosha as a member of the august tribunal.

[43] Cf. Vd. 4. 54–55.

The struggle between the Powers of Good and Evil at the Judgment. Before we turn to the accounts concerning the Chinvat Bridge itself, let us supply one further detail regarding the contest that takes place at the Judgment of the individual soul. If we are correct in interpreting an important passage in the Vidēvdāt, where we are told that in the case of the faithful who perform certain acts of supreme merit

> the Two Spirits (*dva mainyu*) [44] will not enter into contention (*rəna*),[45]

we may infer that in the case of the less pious souls the power of good has to contend against that of evil and with the demoniac hosts who struggle for the possession of the soul. We can well picture Angra Mainyu accusing the souls at the Judgment Seat, while Spenta Mainyu either confirms the accusation or defends his former client.

The important role played by the Chinvat Bridge in the Later Avesta. In more than one passage in the Younger Avesta the Chinvat Bridge is invoked as an object of adoration and worship, which in itself is sufficient to show its importance in Later Zoroastrianism.[46]

As already noted in the previous chapter, the crossing of this Bridge [47] is a matter of supreme moment. The souls of the pious will happily pass the Chinvat Bridge, made by Mazdāh

---

[44] The *dva +mainyū* refer to the two Principles of Good and Evil, *Spənta.°* and *Aŋra.°*. So also Jackson, revising his earlier interpretation in *Hymn of Zoroaster*, p. 26; cf. also Bthl. *AirWb.* 1527.

[45] Vd. 7. 52. Darmesteter seems to regard this as the contest which goes on between the forces of good and evil during the three days and three nights after death (see *SBE.* 4. 89 n. 1). The present writer, however, believes this to be the struggle that takes place immediately prior to the ascent of the soul to Paradise, as mentioned in the following sentence of the text, so that it should be distinguished from the three nights' battle. It is the last desperate attempt on the part of the demons to snatch away the soul of the pious to Hell.

[46] Cf. Sr. 2. 30; 1. 30; Vr. 7. 1; Vd. 19. 36.

[47] The idea is exceedingly elaborated in the Phl. literature, as we shall see in the next chapter.

(*Mazdaðātəm*) and renowned afar (*dūraēsrūtəm*), as we can gather from passages in the Vidēvdāt, the Yasna, and the Vishtāsp Yasht.[48] The Bridge being crossed, they attain to the beatitude of Paradise, the abode of the blest.

In contrast to the picture of the crossing of the Bridge by the righteous in safety, we have the figure of the wicked who will suffer terrible anguish at the transit and will be unable to pass, being destined to fall at the appropriate place into the dark abyss of Hell. The V i d ē v d ā t (13. 8–9) gives a vivid description of the suffering undergone at the Bridge by the souls of the wicked who have committed certain mortal sins. We are told that

> his (namely, the sinner's) soul will go to the other world with louder cries and greater lamentations than the howls of pain [49] a wolf raises when trapped in a very deep pit.[50]
>
> No other soul will help his soul [51] at death [52] in spite of (its) cry and lamentation in (the other) world,[53] nor will the two dogs [54] that keep the Bridge help [55] his soul after death, in spite of (its) cry and lamentation in (the other) world.[56]

[48] Cf. Vd. 19. 30 (see above, p. 66); Ys. 71. 16; VYt. 42; as for Vd. 18. 6, see Bthl. *Zum AirWb.* 168; cf. also Frag. 2 in Vicharkart i Dēnīk as given by Bartholomae in *IF.* 12. 94, cf. also below, page 110.

[49] *vayōi*, interjection, 'woe, alas,' as in Ys. 53. 7; here as a substantive, 'cry of anguish, howls of pain'; cf. Bthl. *AirWb.* 1359.

[50] *razura-*, n., 'pit,' cf. Bthl. *AirWb.* 1515.

[51] Possibly compare the idea in Ys. 45. 11; 46. 10. See also p. 85 below.

[52] *paiti irista*, loc. sg.

[53] Differently Bthl. *AirWb.* 534 (s.v. *xraosya-*), reading as *aŋhe*, 'its.'

[54] Cf. Vd. 19. 30 (see above, p. 36, 65); cf. SD. 31. 5 (see below, p. 107); it is interesting to note a similar idea in Rig-Veda 10. 14. 11: *śvānau . . . rakṣitārau . . . pathirākṣī* (see Kaegi, *Rigveda*, p. 208). See also Bloomfield, *Cerberus, the Dog of Hades*, p. 27–30, Chicago, 1905, and cf. Bthl. *AirWb.* 898.

[55] *bązaiti*, 3d sg. instead of dual, influenced, no doubt, by the same verb in the preceding line.

[56] Vd. 13. 8, 9. For other mortal sins which impede the soul's crossing, cf. Vd. 13. 3 and also the Nikātum-Frag. 2. 14, as given by Darmesteter in *JA.* (1886) 8. 185. See also Bthl. *AirWb.* 596, 692.

Conclusion. Thus the souls of the wicked reap the fruit of their sinful acts in this world and pass on to the next with words of woe and amid tortures of fear and pain. They sink into the depths of Hell, where still greater agony awaits them.

After surveying in detail the Gāthic and the Later Avestan writings concerning an Individual Judgment, let us pass to descriptions contained in the Pahlavi literature.

CHAPTER IX

THE INDIVIDUAL JUDGMENT ACCORDING TO THE PAHLAVI WRITINGS

Introduction. In the last chapter we saw how the writings of the Later Avesta developed and elaborated the lofty ethical ideas and teachings of the Gāthās concerning a *judicium particulare*. The process of embodying the highly abstract and spiritual concepts of the Gāthās in more concrete imagery is carried further in the Pahlavi treatises, which give a vivid description of the judgment scene and its many adjuncts. We shall here follow the broad general outlines laid down in the two previous chapters, and present the Pahlavi account under such main headings as the store of good works in Paradise, the Bridge of Judgment and its location, the judgment scene with its triad of heavenly Judges, the accounting and balancing of the good and bad actions, and the passage of the souls over the Chinvat Bridge.

The store of Good Works. We have seen how the Gāthās speak in unmistakable terms regarding the good works of the faithful which are diligently recorded and treasured up in Ahura's House to be brought to the final reckoning; and practically the same teaching is to be found in the Later Avesta, as we have already noticed. Many allusions to this store of good works (*hanbār i karpak*) are to be found in the Pahlavi books.

The doctrine is summed up in the words of the Dātastān i Mēnūk i Khrat:—

> Be thou diligent in making a store of good works, in order that it may come to thy succor in the spiritual world.[1]

[1] MX. 2. 96, 97; cf. also MX. 22. 6 and Aog. 83.

This is the store of one's own good actions, which, according to an account in the Dātastān i Dēnīk, is carried before the soul in its journey upward by its own Conscience, which comes in the form of a beautiful Maiden and is here termed the 'treasure-bearer' (ganjbar).[2] Similarly, we are told, the Conscience of the wicked, which appears to its soul in the form of an ugly Hag, carries a heavy load which is 'the store of its sin' (hanbār an-š vinās).[3]

This Pahlavi treatise devotes five consecutive chapters [4] to this topic of the store of works, expounding it from different angles. To summarize very briefly, we are here informed that the good works done for the dead man by surviving relatives and others differ in effect from those ordered or done by himself during his lifetime, for the latter go to the account of the setōš [5]

[2] DD. 24. 5, 6; cf. also SVV. 4. 89–99; see above, p. 40, and also below, p. 86.

[3] DD. 25. 5, 6; cf. also ŠVV. 4. 89–99; see above, p. 43, and also below, p. 87.

[4] DD. 8–12.

[5] The word s(e)tōš (Pāz. sēdōš) is a highly technical term, and is used in the Pahlavi and Pāzand writings for the ceremonies performed in honor of Srōsh during the first three days after death; cf. for example, PhlVd. 7. 52 comm.; 8. 22 comm.; 19. 40 comm.; Nīr. 1. 2. 3; 1. 10. B, 3; 2. 2. B, 15; 2. 16. A, 1, 19 (= tr. Bulsara, p. 64, 113, 155, 293, 298); ŠNŠ. 8. 6; 10. 2; 12. 31; DD. 28. 1; 55. 1; 81. 7, 8, 10, 12; PhlRiv. 15. 1 (= ed. Dhabhar, p. 40); Patīt i Pašīmānī, 12. The term is further used to designate the particular period when these ceremonies are performed, that is, the period of the first three days and nights after death; cf. for example, ŠNŠ. 8. 6; 12. 5; DD. 8. 4; 14. 4; 28. 5; Patīt i Īrānī, 4 (= ed. Antia, p. 135). The Nīrangastān twice gives the word stūīh in place of s(e)tōš, a possible oversight on the part of the copyist, who evidently took the word in the sense of 'praise, adoration' (see Nīr. 2. 16. A, 1, 19).

Various conjectures have been made by scholars as to the etymology of this difficult word. West (SBE. 5. 303 n. 1) reads it as satūīh, 'the triplet,' but such an interpretation fails to bring out the full import of the term. Dastur Hoshangji (see his Vendidād, vol. 2, p. 208) understands it as being derived from Av. Sraoša, but such a derivation is highly improbable. The present writer believes that the latter part of the word s(e)tōš is to be connected with Skt. toṣa and NP. tōša, 'sustenance, comfort, satisfaction' (see Hübschmann, Persische Studien, p. 49; Jackson, Early Persian Poetry, p. 11); hence s(e)tōš would mean 'triple satisfaction,' thus referring to the ceremonies performed

and the balance (*hamār i setōš u tarāzūk*), whereas the former are merely for the enjoyment of his soul and do not affect its final destiny.⁶ The sooner good works are done in this world, the better for the destiny of the soul in the hereafter, because there is a continuous growth of merit (*vaxš i karpak*) accruing therefrom, and this is constantly added to the original deposit placed in heaven to one's credit.⁷ We are also informed that at the final reckoning 'the growth of good work' is balanced against 'the growth of sin,' whereas 'the original good' (*būn karpak*) stands up against 'the original sin,' the former in both cases eradicating the latter.⁸

The Treasure-house of Perpetual Profit. The Pahlavi books naturally regard the store of good works (*hanbār i karpak*) as being preserved in the heavenly region. Early in the Pahlavi period we see an attempt made by the translators and commentators of the Avesta to propound this teaching concerning a spiritual treasure-house. They saw the tenet enshrined in the Avestan doctrine of Misvāna Gātu,⁹ which they interpreted as *Hamēšak Sūt Gāh*, 'Place of Perpetual Profit.' The Pahlavi

during the first three days after death. If the Pāzand reading *sēdōš* is more accurate than the Pahlavi *s(e)tōš* (granting that the *t* in the Pahlavi word represents a *d* 'primitif,' as suggested by Darmesteter, *Ét. ir.* 1. 319), it should be connected with the Phl. word *dōš*, 'darkness, evening, night.' Cf. Av. **daošā-* (as in the word *daošatara* of Ys. 57. 29 and Vd. 1. 18; see Bthl. *AirWb.* 674), Skt. *doṣā* (see Macdonell, *Skt. Dictionary*, 2d ed., p. 126), NP. *dōš* (see Horn, *Neupers. Etymologie*, p. 130); in that case *s(e)tōš* would mean 'three nights,' thus referring to the particular period during which the soul is supposed to hover about the body before finally departing for the other world.

⁶ DD. 8. 1–6; 9. 1–4.

⁷ DD. 10. 1–2; cf. also PhlRiv. 28 (ed. Dhabhar, p. 95–97), and later SD. 81. 1–18 (see below, p. 99–100), SDBd. 28. 1–7 (ed. Dhabhar, p. 96–97).

⁸ DD. 11. 1–2; 12. 1–5.

⁹ The Avestan words *misvāna gātav*, 'place of the mixed,' more properly refer to what is indicated in the Gāthās as 'the Separate Place (*nanā*)' (Ys. 48. 4, see above, p. 32), reserved for the souls of those 'whose wrong and whose right deeds balance (*hǝmǝ-myāsaitē*)' (cf. Ys. 33. 1, see above, p. 50), and are to be connected with the well-known Pahlavi term *hamistakān* (cf. PhlVd. 7. 52; AVN. 6. 1–12; IrBd. 30. 13; MX. 7. 18; DD. 20. 3) with which they are etymologically as well as semantically connected. See Bthl. *AirWb.* 1187.

expression, *hamēšak sūt gāh*, occurs for example as a version of *misvāna gātav* in three Avestan passages (namely, Vd. 19. 36; Sr. 1. 30; 2. 30).[10] The Pahlavi translation of the Vidēvdāt passage here mentioned (Vd. 19. 36), together with the commentary, runs as follows:—

> I invoke the Paradise of the righteous, bright and all-blissful. I invoke the Garōtmān, the abode of Ōharmazd, the abode of the Amahraspandān, the abode of <those> other righteous ones. I invoke the sovereign Place of Perpetual Profit <its perpetual profitness (*hamēšak sūtīh*) is this, that till (*tāk*) it becomes (lit. became) a store (*hanbār*), there is (lit. was) continual profit therefrom>; the Chinvat Bridge, created by Ōharmazd, <I also invoke>.[11]

The Pahlavi commentators seem, therefore, to have understood the Avestan concept of Misvāna Gātu as referring to a spiritual treasure-house, or celestial *thesaurus meritorum*, where the good works of the faithful were deposited, bearing perpetual interest (*hamēšak sūt*). Thus there was a continual growth of the store of merits, to be drawn upon by all the faithful, presumably both at the time of the Individual Judgment and also at the final Renovation of the world.[12]

The doctrine concerning the *Hamēšak Sūt Gāh* becomes clearer in the light of the later Pahlavi treatise Dātastān i Dēnīk. Speaking of the nature of Heaven and the happy state of the blessed, the author of that work goes on to say:—

> And there (i.e. in Heaven) is the joy and happiness of the angels from the Place of Perpetual Profit (*hamēšak*

---

[10] The Avestan words are quoted and similarly interpreted also in the Pahlavi commentary on Ys. 19. 1 and Yt. 1. 1.

[11] PhlVd. 19. 36. See Darmesteter, *ZA.* 2. 271 n. 98; and Spiegel, *Commentar über das Avesta*, 1. 448–449 (Vienna, 1864).

[12] For previous discussions of the subject, see Spiegel, *Eranische Alterthumskunde*, vol. 2, p. 16, 17 (Leipzig, 1873); Böklen, *Parsische Eschatologie*, p. 58–59; and Moulton, *EZ.* p. 312–314.

sūt gāh), the abundant and undiminishable Treasury (*ganj*),[13] inexhaustible and boundless.[14]

Here and elsewhere, as shown by the following passages, the treatise expressly speaks of the Place of Perpetual Profit as a Treasure-house with its superabundant store of merit.

For instance, this Pahlavi book states that this *thesaurus meritorum* is situated in Paradise, or more precisely, adjoining the 'Endless Light' (*asar rōšnīh*).[15] Speaking of three realms into which the whole universe was divided according to the earliest creations of Ōharmazd, the author tells us that—

> the one at the top is joined to the Endless Light, in which is the Treasury of Perpetual Profit (*hamēšak sūt ganj*); the one at the bottom reached to the Deepest (i.e. Hell), in which is the Fiend (*druj*) full of evil; and one is between those two thirds (which are) below and above.[16]

The same treatise indicates the close association of the Treasure-house with the Endless Light by mentioning the two side by side twice again.[17]

The Dātastān i Dēnīk develops the idea of the treasury still further when it says that joy, happiness, and supreme reward of a blissful state are meted out to the soul of the righteous from this spiritual Storehouse:—

> His (i.e. a righteous man's) attainment of the recompense (*pātdahišn*) is from the Treasury of Perpetual Profit (*ganj i hamēšak sūt*), the immortal and unlimited, which shall never perish.[18]

---

[13] West translates differently as 'space' (*gunj*), see *SBE*. 18. 57, 70, 121, and 85 n. 5 in particular.
[14] DD. 26. 3.
[15] This is a Pahlavi rendering of the Avestan *anaγra raočå* (see Bthl. *AirWb*. 114–115).
[16] DD. 37. 24.
[17] See DD. 37. 22; 31. 24.
[18] DD. 38. 3; see also later SD. 64. 9; SDBd. 65. 5; see below, page 100.

Another Pahlavi treatise, Shāyist nē-Shāyist, speaks likewise of the spiritual Treasure-house (*ganj*) where the merit accruing from ceremonial worship is accumulated and its store becomes available for the benefit of the souls of the faithful in general.[19]

Repentance and expiation. This teaching of the accumulation of merit leads us to speak of a matter which was a recognized dogma of Sasanian Zoroastrianism. We noted above [20] that the old doctrine of Zarathushtra as set forth in the Gāthās knows nothing of a real remission of sins, but that later Zoroastrianism compromises by allowing repentance and expiation. The Pahlavi books speak of two kinds of renunciation of sin (*patītīh*), the one external and the other internal. To paraphrase the text, the external duty is this, that the sin is to be confessed by the contrite in words (*bē gōbišn*), and the internal or mental duty is this, that the sin is to be renounced with a solemn promise by the penitent in the following words: 'Henceforth I will not commit sin.' [21] Sins both of commission and omission are to be confessed in detail to the high-priest, and the forgiveness of sin will depend largely upon the effectual determination to avoid such offenses in the future.[22] Besides the renunciation of sin, one has to expiate his wrong-doings. The expiation or atonement of sin (*tōčišn*) consists in performing acts of merit so as to heap up the store of good works in the spiritual life-account.[23] Only in this way can his sins be completely remitted.

We are informed, furthermore, that the offenses which have been thus confessed and properly expiated are canceled and are not to be accounted for at the Individual Judgment.[24] But,

---

[19] ŠNŠ. 8. 4; cf. *Āfrīn i Artāk Fravart* 11, also later SD. 1. 5, see below, p. 102.
[20] See page 53, above.
[21] ŠNŠ. 8. 8. The whole chapter is devoted to this subject.
[22] Cf. ŠNŠ. 4. 14; DD. 41. 5; 48. 20; MX. 52. 3; 53. 8; and especially PhlVd. comm. 7. 51–52. See also later SD. 45. 5–11; 84. 1. For the four formulas of confession, as contained in the Parsi prayer-book, see Antia, *Pāzend Texts*, p. 118–152.
[23] Cf. ŠNŠ. 8. 15–16; DD. 12. 2; 15. 5; and especially PhlVd. comm. 7. 53–54.
[24] DD. 13. 2, 3.

on the other hand, the sins and crimes that remain unconfessed and have not been atoned for will be recorded as 'debits' in the life-accounting of the soul, for which it shall undergo severe punishment at the time of the Individual Judgment at the Chinvat Bridge.[25]

It may not be out of place here to mention that the Pahlavi writings divide sins into two great classes, *hamēmār* and *ruvānīk*. A *hamēmār* sin is a secular offense which involves an injury done to a person or an animal, who thereby becomes an 'accuser' (*hamēmār*) and who must be satisfied by an act of atonement before confession is made to the high-priest if the *patītīh* is really to avail to remove the sin.[26] A *ruvānīk* sin, on the other hand, is one which affects only the sinner's own soul and which can be sufficiently atoned for by performing, or causing others to perform, a good work (e.g. a religious ceremony) that produces its effects *ex opere operato*.[27]

The five indispensable Good Works. The Pahlavi book Shāyist nē-Shāyist already mentioned speaks at length on the subject of the merit and sin which 'go to the Bridge' and are taken into account at the individual judgment. According to this treatise, following the Nīrangastān section [28] of the old Huspāram Nask,[29] numerous acts of duty are enjoined upon the faithful; chief among these is the celebration of five important and indeed indispensable ceremonies. These five are the rites performed at the season-festivals (*gāsānbār*),[30] those on the third

---

[25] DD. 24. 5-6.

[26] Cf. ŠNŠ. 8. 1, 14-17; DD. 14. 3; PhlVd. comm. 3. 35, 42; 4. 4; 13. 2; also SD. 42. 1-7; 63. 11. For a discussion of this legal term, as employed in the Sasanian Code, see Bartholomae, 'Zum sasanidischen Recht,' part 1, p. 21; 2, p. 49-50 (*Sitzungsberichte Heidelb. Akad. Wiss.* 5 [1918], Abh. 14).

[27] Cf. ŠNŠ. 8. 1, 16; DD. 14. 3.

[28] See Nīr. 2. 2, appendix B 15-16 (= tr. Bulsara, p. 155-156).

[29] The seventeenth Nask in order, as given in Dk. 8. 28-37. For the Nīrangastān section see Dk. 8. 29.

[30] The Season Festivals are six in number. See Gray, 'Der Iranische Kalender,' in Jackson's *Die iranische Religion*, in *GIrPh*. 2. 676; cf. also Modi, *Religious Ceremonies*, p. 446-455.

day of the first month (*rapiθwin*),³¹ on the three days after a death (*setōš*),³² on the days devoted to the guardian spirits (*fravartīkān*),³³ and the periodical veneration of the sun and moon. Performed at the appropriate times they redound to the advantage of the soul in the hereafter. Any omission in properly performing these five is a sin which must be accounted for at the *judicium particulare*.³⁴

The Chinvat Bridge and its location. Before we pass to the *judicium particulare*, at which a statement of the soul's life-account is made out, and before we describe the passage of the soul over the Bridge, let us determine, so far as possible, the presumable location of this Bridge of the Separator according to the Pahlavi books. The silence of the Gāthās on the point is easy to understand; and even the Later Avestan texts are far from explicit here, though its association with *Harā bərəzaitī* (Alburz) in the Vidēvdāt is very significant.³⁵ When we come to our later authorities in Pahlavi literature, we find the Bridge somewhat more definitely localized.

According to the Pahlavi books, the Chinvat Bridge is conceived of as being somewhere in Media. We are told that it goes from the northern foot of *Harburz* (Alburz) to the top of its southern ridge, and underneath its center, which rests on the 'Peak of Judgment' (*čikāt i dāitīk*), lies Hell.³⁶ We are further informed that the Peak of Judgment (and thus necessarily Hell) is in the middle of the world,³⁷ in Ērān Vēž, the primeval home

³¹ See Modi, *op. cit.* p. 458.
³² See above, page 73, note 5.
³³ See below, p. 105, and Modi, *op. cit.* p. 465-479.
³⁴ ŠNŠ. 12. 31; 13. 29. Cf. also Dk. 8. 29. 1; 9. 49. 8; PhlRiv. 15. 1-15 (ed. Dhabhar, p. 40-43); Patīt i Pašīmānī, 9, 12; and also later SD. 6. 1-7, see below, pages 100-101.
³⁵ See above, pages 63, 66.
³⁶ IrBd. 30. 1; Bd. 30. 33; AVN. 3. 1; and see Bthl. *AirWb.* 597. According to PhlVd. 19. 30 comm., the Chinvat Bridge stretches over Hell between the divine Mount Harburz and the Peak of Judgment (cf. also Dk. 9. 20. 3; DD. 21. 2).
³⁷ Bd. 12. 7; AVN. 53. 1. In a short Pahlavi text entitled *Apar Čīm i Drōn*, 'Concerning the meaning of Drōn (sacred cake),' the cake itself is com-

of Mazdāh-worship,[38] which the Bundahishn places somewhere in northern Persia 'in the direction of Āturpātkān.'[39] The river Dāitīk is also found in this region, which is the scene of Zarathushtra's first promulgation of the religion.[40] If we may hazard a conjecture, a mountain situated in this territory which could possibly have captured the popular imagination as the Peak of Judgment would be the magnificent Mount Damāvand. It is of interest to note that Damāvand was at one time a volcano, and that the overflowing molten lava perhaps suggested the awful picture of the hissing and roaring hell-fire. 'The neck of Arezūr,'[41] which is called 'the gate of Hell,'[42] may well suggest the idea of a crater, here that of the extinct or dormant volcanic mountain Damāvand. Thus we may conceive of the Chinvat Bridge as spanning Mount Damāvand, the most imposing peak of the Alburz range, and we may picture the very middle part of the Bridge, which is its most crucial part,[43] as stretching over the gaping crater of the active volcano, or Hell itself.

The Judgment at the Chinvat Bridge: the reckoning and the weighing. We have already spoken at length in the two preceding chapters regarding the general conception of this belief, and have attempted to show that it forms part of the ethical and eschatological system of the Gāthās and the Later Avesta with their teaching of the responsibility of man to account for his deeds and their doctrine of the audit of the soul.

pared to the earth, its border round about to the Harburz Mountain encircling the world, and the $gāuš\ hu\delta\mathring{a}$ (clarified butter) placed in its middle is likened to the Čikāt i Dāitīk, 'Peak of Judgment.' (For the text and translation see Kaikhusro D. J. J. Asa, 'The Symbolism of the Darun,' *Hoshang Memorial Volume*, p. 201–205. Cf. also the text given in PhlRiv. 56. 1–8, ed. Dhabhar, p. 166–167).

[38] Dk. 9. 20. 3; DD. 21. 2.
[39] Bd. 29. 12.
[40] Bd. 20. 13, 32; 32. 3.
[41] The *arəzūrahe grīvaya* of Vd. 3. 7; Phl. transcribes as *arzūr grīvak*. Cf. Modi, 'Mount Arezūra of the Avesta, a Volcanic Mountain,' in *Spiegel Memorial Volume*, Bombay, 1908, p. 188–196.
[42] Bd. 3. 27; 12. 8; 28. 18; DD. 33. 5; PhlRiv. 50 (ed. Dhabhar, p. 162).
[43] IrBd. 30. 1; DD. 21. 2, 7.

To summarize briefly the main elements comprised in the tenet, all actions, good or bad, done on earth are recorded in heaven; they are the **items** (*dāθra*) which a man puts down to the account of his soul and in accordance with which he will be judged when his reckoning is made up and his account is audited, or—as the Pahlavi literature has it—when his merits and demerits are placed in the **balance** and **weighed** one against the other.[44]

This accounting of the good works (*karpak*) and sin (*vinās*) is also called 'the account of the soul' (*hamār i ruvān*).[45] We are told that at this 'wondrous accounting' (*škaft hamār*),[46] the good and evil deeds are justly accounted for (*rāstihā hamārīhēt*).[47]

The accounting—the method by which the Individual Judg-

---

[44] Although found in Egypt and elsewhere, this is a fundamental tenet also of Zoroastrian eschatology. A passage from Herodotus may be cited in support of the antiquity of the belief as thoroughly Iranian (see Hdt. 1. 137; cf. above, p. 54).

As has been noted already, Zoroastrianism, especially of the Pahlavi period, exerted extensive influence upon Manichaean eschatology, and it is therefore natural to look for some trace of this doctrine in the Manichaean Fragments. Professor Jackson (*JAOS.* 43. 20–22) draws attention to such an allusion to the balance in one of the Turkish Manichaean Fragments brought back by Le Coq from Chotscho. The passage considered occurs in Le Coq, *Türkische Manichaica aus Chotscho II*, p. 12, Fragment T. II. D. 173, recto, lines 7–12 (*Abh. Akad. Wiss. Berlin*, 1919), and the designation for the scales in Turkish, *t(a)razuk*, corresponds to the familiar Pahlavi word *tarāzūk*, NP. *tarāzū*. The Turkish text reads as follows (lines 6–12):

> 'The just judge seizes the confused
> soul which appears
> as in a mirror. In the **balance**
> it is placed down, it is said.
> If the **balance** rises, its deeds . . . (?)
> its evil done
> deeds will . . . (?)' [*the broken text here renders the sense uncertain*]

[*End of the page; the reverse page contains the ensuing torments for the damned.*]

[45] DD. 8. 6; GŠ. 133.
[46] DD. 22. 2.
[47] DD. 24. 5.

ment is effected in part—takes place on the dawn following the third night after death,[48] or, as it is sometimes said, 'in the *setōš*.' [49] The souls, we are told, go to the account at the light of dawn in the period of Ōshahīn.[50]

As to the place where the accounting is made, we are informed that it is on Mount Harburz (Alburz).[51] The Bundahishn expressly mentions that the Judges take account of the soul at the 'Peak of Judgment' (*čikāt i dāitīk*), which is in the middle of the world, on which stands the Chinvat Bridge.[52] Combining the evidence presented by these statements we can safely say that the soul renders its account at the Chinvat Bridge, which is situated on Mount Harburz.[53]

The judges who reckon the account are Mihr, Srōsh, and Rashnū. The Pahlavi books give us an elaborate description of their functions and present a vivid picture of the celestial trial. Mihr, the first of this divine triad, is concerned as the genius of light and truth, the friend and helper of the just, but the stern chastiser of those who break their pledge or are in any way untruthful.[54] The second divinity is Srōsh, who stands by and keeps guard,[55] while the third, Rashnū, holds with exactness the balance in which the good and bad actions are weighed. Other angels are present, but demons likewise lurk about, eager to seize upon the soul. The best picture of the *judicium particulare* is given in the Pahlavi Dātastān i Mēnūk i Khrat.

[48] DD. 13. 2; 20. 3.
[49] DD. 28. 5.
[50] DD. 30. 3. Ōshahīn is the period extending from midnight until the stars disappear at dawn. DD. 32. 4 states that the account is rendered in 'the fourth night after passing away.' So also the later work SD. (1. 4). The statements of these two works cannot be regarded as strictly accurate in the light of numerous other passages.
[51] DD. 20. 3.
[52] Bd. 12. 7; cf. also Dk. 8. 14. 8.
[53] For other passages concerning the location of the Bridge of Judgment, see above, pages 79–80.
[54] Dk. 9. 20. 4; DD. 14. 3. Cf. especially for the three judges Dk. 8. 44. 16.
[55] DD. 28. 6.

ACCORDING TO THE PAHLAVI WRITINGS 83

The passages here presented, first with reference in particular to the soul of the righteous, read as follows:—

(115) And the fourth day, in the light of the dawn—with the co-operation of Srōsh the righteous, Vāy the good,[56] Vahrām the strong,[57] and with the opposition of Astvidāt,[58] Vāy the bad,[59] the demon Frēhzīsht, the demon Nīzīsht,[60] and the evil-designing activity of the mischief-worker Ēshm,[61] of the wounding spear—[the soul] goes [62] up to the awesome, exalted Chinvat Bridge—to which every one, righteous and wicked, goes.

(116–117) And many opponents are lurking there (*pāt ēstēnd*) with the mischievous design of Ēshm of the wounding spear, and Astvidāt, who devours creatures of every kind, and knows no satiety (*sērīh*).

(118–122) And there is the mediation (*mīyān-čikīh*) of Mihr and Srōsh and Rashnū, and the weighing (*tarāzīnītarīh*) of Rashnū the just, on the balance of the Spirits (*tarāzūk i mēnūkān*)

---

[56] This associate of Srōsh is the genius of pure air, invoked particularly in Yt. 15, and mentioned elsewhere in the Later Avesta. See Bthl. *AirWb.* 1357; cf. also DD. 30. 4; ŠNŠ. 11. 4; 17. 4.

[57] The genius of victory of the Later Avesta. Yt. 14 is dedicated to him. See Bthl. *AirWb.* 1421–1422; cf. also Bd. 27. 24; ŠNŠ. 22. 20.

[58] Transcription of Av. *Astō.vīδātav*, the demon of death who binds the parting soul; cf. Vd. 5. 8; see Bthl. *AirWb.* 214; cf. also Bd. 28. 35; DD. 37. 51–52.

[59] The demon of contaminated air, *Vāy i vattar*, as opposed to *Vāy i vēh*. He is mentioned in Vd. 5. 8; see Bthl. *AirWb.* 1358; cf. also DD. 30. 4; 37. 44, 52.

[60] These demons have not been recognized elsewhere, as West rightly observes. See *SBE.* 24. 17 n. 5.

[61] The demon of wrath, the *Aēšma(daēva)* of the Avesta, and the *Asmodeus* of the Book of Tobit (3. 8, 17). Frequently mentioned in Avestan and Pahlavi literature. See Bthl. *AirWb.* 35–36.

[62] Literally, 'is a goer.'

[63] Regarding the reading of this problematic word, see Junker, in *Dastur Hoshang Memorial Volume*, p. 392–394.

which renders no favor (*hangrād*)⁶³ on either side, neither for the righteous nor yet for the wicked, neither for the independent rulers (*xᵛatāyān*) nor yet for the rulers of a country (*dēhəpatān*). As much as a hair's breadth it will not turn, and is no respecter (of persons),⁶⁴ and him who is an independent ruler and (him who is) ruler of a country it considers equally, in (its) decision (*dātəstān*), with him who is the least of mankind.⁶⁵

Thus perfect justice is meted out to every soul. The high and the low are equal in the eye of divine justice. The only thing that is taken into consideration is the sum of the good and evil deeds that the individual has done during his life on earth.

As noted above, this description of the judgment scene, though having special reference to the righteous soul,⁶⁶ is in a more general aspect applicable to all, the righteous and the wicked alike. And it is for this reason that the celestial trial scene in the case of the **wicked** soul is described rather summarily, though not without additional touches. The passage (MX. 2. 161–163) runs as follows:—

(161–162) The fourth day the demon Vīzarsh⁶⁷ comes and binds the soul of the wicked with the very evil noose (*vattar band*), and, with the opposition of Srōsh the righteous, he leads (it) up to the Chinvat Bridge.

⁶⁴ *āzarm nē dārēt*, lit. 'keeps no dignity,' i.e. does not take into consideration the high or low station to which the individual to be judged belonged during life on earth.

⁶⁵ MX. 2. 115–122.

⁶⁶ The sections of MX. 2. 114–157 deal with the fates of the righteous soul, and sections 158–194 describe the destiny of the wicked soul.

⁶⁷ A direct transcription of Av. *Vīzarəša*; see above, p. 63 n. 21, and also p. 24, 38. In the Phl. literature the demon is also mentioned in Bd. 28. 18; DD. 32. 4, 7; 37. 44.

⁶⁸ *āškārak kūnēt*, 'makes apparent, visible,' i.e. lays open, exposes. Ner. Skt. vers. has *prakaṭam kurute*. West (*SBE*. 24. 22) translates as 'detects.'

ACCORDING TO THE PAHLAVI WRITINGS

(163) Then Rashnū the just exposes [68] the soul of the wicked for (its) wickedness (*pa darvandīh*).[69]

Though the text is far from being explicit, the sense at any rate is clear. Rashnū's scales in the case of the wicked reveal a decided preponderance of the works of iniquity over those of merit. The lost soul is accordingly condemned to perdition and torture by the decision of the divine judges.

The same treatise further describes how the demon Vīzarsh grabs the soul of the wicked once more and beats it unmercifully. The soul weeps bitterly and cries for help. But, alas, all its struggles and all its supplications are in vain; neither the divinities nor the demons come to its assistance.[70] And this is the mere beginning of the frightful fate that awaits the wicked soul.

The Artāk Vīrāz Nāmak also speaks of the weighing of the souls by Rashnū, and mentions the company of angels in connection therewith:—

(2–3) With the assistance of Srōsh the righteous and Ātar the angel, I passed over easily, happily, stout-heartedly and triumphantly, on the Chinvat Bridge. (I had) much protection from Mihr the angel, and Rashnū the just, Vāy the good, and the angel Vahrām the strong, and Ashtāt [71] the angel, the world-increaser, . . .

(5) I also saw, I Artāk Vīrāz, Rashnū the just, who held in his hand the yellow golden balance (*tarāzūk i zart i zarrēn*), and weighed (*handāčēt*) [72] the righteous and the wicked.[73]

---

[69] MX. 2. 161–163.
[70] MX. 2. 164–166.
[71] Transcription of Av. *Arštāt*, the goddess of Uprightness, who is closely associated with Rashnū. Both are invoked in the prayer appointed for the *ōšahīn* period of the day, cf. DD. 30. 3, and note 50 above.
[72] Literally, (present for imperf.) 'considers, deliberates upon, decides, passes judgment on.'
[73] AVN. 5. 2–5; cf. also West and Haug, *Book of Arda Viraf*, p. 155–156.

86 THE INDIVIDUAL JUDGMENT

In this connection may be noticed the fact that the three special offerings of the consecrated cakes (*drōn*) are made [74] on the dawn of the fourth day (*čahārom*), when the soul stands at the individual judgment. The first offering is dedicated to Rashnū and Ashtāt, the second to Vāy the good, and the third to *Artāk Fravart*, or the holy Fravashi of the departed person,[75] together with those of all righteous persons who have lived in this world from the time of Gayōmart (i.e. the first man on earth), and also of those that will live until the coming of the Saoshyant and the final renovation of the world. It is easy to understand the propitiatory import of this triple oblation.[76]

Closely associated with the accounting is the meeting of the soul with the bearer of its deeds, good or bad, as the case may be. The Dātastān i Dēnīk furnishes interesting details as follows:—

> The same third night, at the arrival of dawn,[77] the treasure-bearer (*ganjbar*) of good works, like a beautiful maiden (*hučihr kanīk*) [78] comes out to meet [the soul] with the store of its own good works (*hanbār i x^{v}ēšak karpak*); and the witch-collected [79] unexpiated

---

[74] These are technically known as the Bāj (*Vāč*) or Drōn ceremonies. For a detailed description of these ceremonies and allied matters, see below, page 103, note 24.

[75] It is to be noted that among the Parsis of today an additional Drōn ceremony is performed in honor of Srōsh. This further propitiation of Srōsh is natural owing to the important role he plays as the protector of the soul. No ceremony, however, appears to be offered to Mithra at this period.

[76] Cf. PhlVd. 8. 22 comm., ŠNŠ. 17. 4; DD. 30. 1–4; 81. 14. Consult West, *SBE.* 5, p. 383, n. 5; see also Modi, *Religious Ceremonies*, p. 78–79, 84–85.

[77] Reading *andar bāmīk āyāft*, following mss. J2, H, DF; see ed. Anklesaria, p. 50 n. 17.

[78] A conception similar to that of the Daēnā, discussed fully in a preceding chapter. See especially p. 39–41, and note AVN. 4. 15–36; MX. 2. 125–144.

[79] The text has *p r d k n č n d*, which West reads (*SBE.* 18. 54) as *parīkōčind*, 'collected by witches.' The latter word, however, seems doubtful; one would expect it to be written *čīnīt*.

(*atōxt*) sins and crimes come to the account (and) are justly accounted for.[80]

Or again, if the soul happens to be that of a wicked person, its store of sins is borne by a hideous woman and carried to the place of accounting:—

> And the third night, at the arrival of dawn, its sin in the form of a woman (*čarāitīk*),[81] frightful, polluted, and tormenting,[82] comes to meet [the soul] with the store of its sin (*hanbār an-š vinās*) and a stinking northerly [83] wind comes out to meet (it), and it comes on shudderingly, quiveringly,[84] and unwillingly, running to the a c c o u n t.[85]

Somewhat different is the description given in the well-known Pahlavi treatise S h k a n d - v i m ā n ī k V i c h ā r, which seems to imply that each soul has two treasure-bearers (*ganjbarān*), the one of its good works and the other of its sins. These treasure-bearers, we are told, proceed to the place of judgment and enter into a contest for the ultimate possession of the soul. The description given here adds further color to the picture of the trial scene as a whole; it runs as follows:—

> (91–92) And the soul is accountable (*hamārōmand*) for its own deeds. Its treasure-bearers (*ganjbarān*), unto whom its good works and sin are entrusted, also advance t h e r e (i.e. to the place of accounting) for a c o n t e s t.

---

[80] DD. 24. 5.

[81] Transcription of Av. *čarāitī-*, though here used of a bad woman, contrary to the Avestan usage; cf. Bthl. *AirWb.* 581.

[82] A conception similar to that of the Daēnā, who comes to greet the soul of the wicked in the form of an ugly hag. See above, p. 41–43, and especially AVN. 17. 10–26.

[83] That is, from the region of hell, as already noted.

[84] Thus West (*SBE.* 18. 56), but, as he says, the rendering is doubtful.

[85] DD. 25. 5.

(93–94) When the treasure-bearer of the good works is of greater strength, by her victory she releases (*bōjēt*) it from the clutches of the accuser,[86] (and) leads [87] it to the Great Enthronement and to the co-relationship (*hamx^vēšīh*) [88] with the luminaries,[89] and it is assisted forever in happy progress.

(95–96) And when the treasure-bearer of its sin is of greater strength, by her victory it is snatched away from the hands of the helper (*ayāwār*),[90] and is consigned to the place of thirst and hunger and to the agonizing abode [91] of disease (*vīmārəstān*).[92]

The evidence is sufficient to show that the scene of the final accounting of the individual soul is filled with many a stirring incident. On the death of a person the powers of good and evil come into sharp conflict. The struggle goes on for three days and three nights, till the judges intervene on the dawn of the fourth day, when the fate of the soul is ultimately decided.

A notable chapter in the Dātastān i Dēnīk admirably describes who are the 'takers of the account' (*hamār-*

---

[86] Here 'the accuser' is not the party injured, but the treasurer of sin, who represents, as it were, all the accusers.

[87] *ārāwēt* (*a r a p d t*). Better adopt Pāz. *ārāmēt* of ms. JE (see ed. Hoshang and West, p. 29 n. 2), a later form of Phl. *ahrāmēt*, 'leads onward.' Cf. ŠVV. 16. 22 (Pāz. *aharāminend*). The word *ahrāmēd* occurs in the Manichaean TPhl. fragments, especially in the sense of 'leading upward' to heaven (e.g. F. W. K. Müller, *Handschriften-Reste*, 2, p. 19 top; Salemann, *Manichäische Studien*, 1, p. 51). West, on the contrary, here translates as 'settles.' The word *ahrāmīhat* (present passive), 'is led,' occurs also in MX. 2. 145, and is used in connection with the soul's being led into the three grades of Heaven. See Junker's note, *Dastur Hoshang Memorial Volume*, p. 394–396.

[88] West (*SBE*. 24. 137) translates as 'mutual delightfulness.'

[89] Referring to the star, moon, and sun stations through which the soul passes on its way to heaven (cf. Bd. 12. 1; DD. 34. 3; MX. 7. 9–11), or more probably it refers by implication to the occupants of heaven, the souls of the righteous, who are said to be luminous and each seated on a throne (cf. AVN. 7–10).

[90] That is, the treasurer of good works.

[91] Referring to hell.

[92] ŠVV. 4. 91–96, cf. above, page 73.

karān) of the good works and sins, both during the lifetime of a person and at the individual judgment and lastly at the general resurrection. The exposition given (DD. 14. 2–5) by the author in answer to a question on this point runs as follows:—

> (2) The reply is this, that Vahūman the archangel takes an account concerning the doers of actions as to good works (and) sin, three times each day while the doer of the action is living,[93] because the taking account of thoughts, words, and deeds of the whole material world is among his duties (*x*^v*ēš.kārīh*).
>
> (3) Concerning the sin (involving) 'accusers' (*hamēmārān*)[94] which is committed by (*ō*) the promise-breakers, Mihr is said (to be), even during the material existence (*gēhīkīh*), over the bodies, words, and fortunes (*hūbaxtak*) of the promise-breakers; as to the amount (*čandīh*) and also as to the time-limit (*tākīh*) <that is, the period when (there is) the adjustment>,[95] Mihr is the taker of account (*hamārkar*).
>
> (4) In the *setōš*, Srōsh the righteous[96] and Rashnū the just are over the reckoning (*patmān*)[97] of good works (and) of sin <the measuring (*sāmān*) of righteousness and wickedness>.[98]
>
> (5) In the future body (*pa tan i pasīn*),[99] on the

---

[93] In the Vishtāsp Yasht (§ 41) Zarathushtra admonishes his royal patron to attend diligently to the task of caring for the beneficent cattle three times a day. Since one of Vahūman's chief functions is the protection of cattle, the idea is that thrice daily he will put such good action to the account of the individual.

[94] This technical term has been fully explained on p. 78, above.

[95] This refers to debts and promises to pay, as is pointed out also by West (*SBE.* 18. 33).

[96] Cf. also DD. 28. 5, 6, where Srōsh is mentioned as one of those who take the account in the *setōš*.

[97] Av. *paitimāna, Skt. *pratimāna*, and NP. *paimān*.

[98] West translates somewhat differently: '. . . over the estimate of the limits of the good works (and) sin of righteousness and wickedness.'

[99] That is, at the time of the resurrection.

completion of every account, Ōharmazd the creator himself takes the account,[100] to whom every account of the *setōš*—all the thoughts, words, and deeds of the creatures—is manifest in His omniscient wisdom.[101]

The author, therefore, in the above passage explicitly indicates who are the makers of the account, and in a later chapter he sums up as follows:—

> ... Those who take the account (*hamārkarān*) are Ōharmazd, Vahūman, Mihr, Srōsh, (and) Rashnū; they shall make up the account (*hamār kūnēt*) of all with justice (*rāstihā*), each one at his own time. . . .[102]

By way of conclusion we may quote two passages from the Pahlavi literature which speak about the threefold destiny that is meted out to the souls according to their deserts at this Individual Judgment. The Dātastān i Mēnūk i Khrat clearly points out that—

> the place of (him) whose good work is more (than his sin) is in Heaven (*vahišt*); the place of (him) whose good work and sin (*karpak u vinās*) are equal is in Hamistakān; and when the sin is more (than the good work), his path is then to Hell (*dōžax*ᵛ).[103]

Or again, as the Artāk Vīrāz Nāmak has it:—

> ... Everyone whose good works are three *srōšō.-čaranām* [104] more than his sin, (goes) to Heaven; (every-

---

[100] This refers undoubtedly to the *judicium universale* when there will occur the three days' separation (Av. *vīdāiti*) of the wicked from the righteous after the assembly of the Satvāstārān; cf. Bd. 30. 10–16; ŠNŠ. 8. 7.
[101] DD. 14. 2–5; cf. also Dk. (ed. Sanjana) 3. 302; MX. 12. 12.
[102] DD. 31. 11.
[103] MX. 12. 13–15; cf. also Dk. 8. 14. 8; ŠNŠ. 6. 2, 3.
[104] A transcription of Av. *sraošō.čaranā-*, cf. Bthl. *AirWb.* 1636, 1637. It is here taken as the name of a very small weight, the exact value of which, according to Haug and West (see *Book of Arda Viraf*, p. 157 n. 3), is no longer

one) whose sin is more, (goes) to Hell; (whereas he) in whom both are equal, remains in the Hamistakān till the future body (i.e. the time of the resurrection).[105]

The judgment of the soul having been rendered at the heavenly tribunal, the next step in the spirit-journey, before it finally reaches its destined goal, is the crossing of the Chinvat Bridge. A detailed description of this crossing is given in the Pahlavi books.

The passage of the soul over the Chinvat Bridge. According to the Pahlavi writings, following the account given in the Avesta,[106] the righteous and the wicked alike must cross the Chinvat Bridge, passing to bliss or perdition, as the case may be.[107]

The difficulties of the passage over this 'Brig o'Dread' are often alluded to and dilated upon in the Pahlavi books. Their teaching is that the Bridge becomes broad or narrow according to the nature of the soul that steps upon it, presenting to the righteous a pathway nine spears (*nēzak*) or twenty-seven arrows (*nāδ*) or a league (*frasang*) in breadth; but it turns to the godless man a sharp edge (*tāy i tēž*), like that of a sword (*šapšēr*) or a razor (*ōstarak*), so that his soul, when half-way across, falls into the abyss of Hell.

The Iranian Bundahishn (30. 1, 9–13), to begin with, gives an elaborate account not only of the nature of the Bridge itself, but also of the actual crossing by the souls of the dead. The description runs as follows:—

known. But we are told in the Shāyist nē-Shāyist (11. 2) that one *srōšō.čaranām* is equivalent to a *dirham* and two *dānk*, and that three *srōšō.čaranām* are the weight of four *dirham* and two *dānk*; consequently, 1 *srōšō.čaranām* = 6 *dānk*. For the word *dānk* (*mad*) cf. Junker, *Frahang i Pahlavīk*, p. 114. See also Darmesteter, *ZA*. 2. introd. p. 17, 20.

[105] AVN. 6. 9–11; cf. also PhlVd. 7. 54 comm.
[106] Cf. especially Vd. 19. 29.
[107] GŠ. 133; HAM. 139, 147; MX. 2. 115. There is a possibility that the idea of the Chinvat Bridge may have been preserved in Manichaeism, if we may judge from a reference to a 'bridge' in a Turkish Manichaean Fragment (Le Coq, *Türk. Manich.* 3, p. 47), see W. Bang, *Muséon*, 36. 235–236.

THE INDIVIDUAL JUDGMENT

(1) . . . In that middle place (i.e. the middle part of the Bridge, situated on the *Cikāt i dāitīk*), there is a sharp edge (*tāy i tēž*)[108] which stands like a sword (*šapšēr*), whose length and breadth are of the height (or extent) of nine spears (*nēzak*)[109]; and there stand the spiritual Yazats, who purify spiritually the souls of the righteous; and (there is also) a spiritual dog (*sak 1*) at the head (*sar*)[110] of the Bridge; and Hell is below the Bridge.

(9a) Then the soul is carried to the base of Mount Harburz <that is, to the very edge of the ridge (*gūk*)[111]>; to the summit (*bālist*) of the Chikāt it goes up, where stands the sharp edge.[112]

(9b) Then, if it be righteous, the sharp edge stands in its breadth (i.e. presents its broad side.)[113] The victorious fire Farnbag[114] dispels (lit. strikes) the darkness; the soul passes over the edge in the form of fire. Thereupon the spiritual Yazats purify it; spiritually it passes over the ridge to the summit of Harburz. Then the good Vāy takes it by the hand and carries it to its

---

[108] Compare NP. *tēz-tāy*, 'keen edge' of a sword or hatchet (see Steingass, *Pers.-Eng. Dictionary*, p. 342). The word *tāy* occurs in the sense of 'edge' in PhlVd. 14. 7 (*tēž-tāy*); DD. 20. 4; 21. 3, 5; and in the sense of 'end' in PhlVd. 19. 6.

[109] A unit of linear measure, equivalent to about 14 feet. Thus the Bridge would be approximately 126 feet wide; for further discussion on the point see below, page 94, note 125, page 95, note 128.

[110] We might conjecturally render 'at (each) end,' because in Vd. 13. 9 we have mention of two dogs who guard the Chinvat Bridge.

[111] Doubtful. Compare the possible NP. equivalent *kūk*, 'dome, cupola' (see Steingass, *Pers.-Eng. Dict.* p. 1063); cf. also Modi, 'An Untranslated Chapter of the Bundehesh,' *JBBRAS*. 21. 56 n. 17, 62 n. 46.

[112] Modi does not divide the section here, and fails to notice that the description so far applies both to the righteous and the wicked. What follows pertains to the righteous alone.

[113] This sentence is to be found in Anklesaria's text, but is omitted by Modi.

[114] One of the great sacred fires of ancient Iran, often mentioned in the Pahlavi literature; see especially Bd. 17. 5–8; VZsp. 11. 8–10; ŠNŠ. 13. 26. On the different sacred fires, see especially Jackson, *JAOS*. 41. 81–106.

own place; the soul is consigned to the place which is in accordance with its own choice. . . .[115]

(10) If the soul be wicked, when it comes from the ridge (*gūk*) over to the Chikāt, that sharp edge (*tāy i tēž*) stands with the same edge (i.e. continues to stand edgewise), and does not give a passage (*vitarg nē dahēt*); and it is obliged against its will (*akāmakīhā*) to walk over the same edge. With three steps which it takes forward—which are the evil thoughts (*dušmat*), evil words (*dušuxt*), and evil deeds (*dušvaršt*) that it has performed—it is cut down (*burīnēt*) [116] from the head (*sar*) of the Bridge, and falls headlong to Hell, and experiences (lit. sees) all kinds of afflictions.[117]

The same notable chapter goes on to give another account of the crossing, namely, that the soul of the righteous is guided over the Bridge by its own Daēnā (conscience) in the form of a lovely damsel,[118] and is led by three steps, which are its good thoughts (*hūmat*), good words (*hūxt*), and good deeds (*hvaršt*), to the resplendent Garōtmān. But if the soul is wicked, it is met by the Conscience of its evil deeds, which commands it to walk over the sharp edge of the Bridge. The wicked soul cries out that it would rather be cut to pieces by a sharp knife (*kārt*) or be pierced by an arrow (*tiγr*) or be utterly annihilated, than be forced to walk over the keen edge. Then its evil actions assume the form of a wild beast (*dat i*). The soul is so terrified that it tries to cross, but at the third step it falls headlong into Hell.[119]

[115] Literally, 'as the soul chooses, there he (i.e. the good Vāy) consigns it,' i.e. in accordance with its deserts.

[116] Modi, *op. cit.* p. 63, has *bardanēt*, 'retires.'

[117] IrBd. 30. 1, 9–10 (= ed. Anklesaria, p. 199, lines 7–10; p. 202, line 10, to p. 203, line 9).

[118] See above, page 40.

[119] IrBd. 30. 11-13. The three sentences that follow in § 13 refer to the destiny of the souls that are consigned to the Hamistakān, and should accordingly be separated as a new section.

THE INDIVIDUAL JUDGMENT

It may be observed here, in regard to the figures which meet the soul at the Bridge, that other Pahlavi accounts represent the soul of the righteous as crossing the Chinvat Bridge with the help of Srōsh the righteous as its ministering angel,[120] whereas the soul of the wicked is dragged to Hell by the tormenting fiend Vīzarsh.[121]

The other text which contains a detailed account of the Bridge and the crossing is the theological treatise Dātastān i Dēnīk. The passage (DD. 21. 2-8) is worth quoting at length; parallels to be found in other Pahlavi works are adduced in the footnotes:—

(2) . . . Reaching unto the vicinity of the Peak of Judgment (čikāt i dāitīk) is the spiritual Chinvat Bridge in the form of a blade (dār karp),[122] which is thrown (across) from the Harburz enclosure (var) back to the Peak of Judgment.

(3) The Bridge (pūhl) is in the semblance of a blade (dār) of many sides (vas pāhlūk), of whose surfaces (pušt)[123] one is broad and the other is thin (bārīk) and sharp (tēž). Its broad surface (sūkīhā)[124] is so large that its width is twenty-seven arrows (nāδ),[125] and its sharp surface is so contracted (tang) that in thinness it is just like the edge (tāy) of a razor (ōstarak).

---

[120] Aog. 8–9; MX. 2. 123–124.

[121] MX. 2. 164–166.

[122] Taking it from Av. *dārā*, Skt. *dhārā*, 'edge.' Thus it becomes synonymous with *tāy*, 'edge,' mentioned above; see page 92. For the mention of *dārā*, 'edge,' in the Avesta, cf. Vd. 14. 7; Yt. 10. 96, 131. See also Bthl. *AirWb.* 739. West (*SBE.* 18. 48) translates the word as 'beam.'

[123] Compare such expressions in New Persian as *pušt i zamīn*, 'the surface of the earth,' *pušt i nāf*, 'the surface of the navel,' etc. See Steingass, *Pers.-Eng. Dictionary*, p. 251; West translates as 'edge.'

[124] Doubtful. West translates as 'sides.'

[125] A measure of distance, equivalent to $5\frac{1}{3}$ *pāδ* (see DD. 43. 5). According to Frahang i Oīm § 27a, *pāδ* is 'fourteen finger-breadths (14 *angušt*),' or about $10\frac{1}{2}$ inches (see Reichelt, *WZKM.* 14. 211; 15. 147). Consequently a *nāδ* would be about 4 feet 8 inches. So also West (see *SBE.* 18. 48 n. 5).

(4) And when the souls of the righteous and the wicked arrive, it turns (*gartēt*) to that side (*gyāk*)[126] which is (suitable to) their requirements (*nīyāzakīhā*).

(5) Through the great glory of the Creator and the command of him who is the just Judge (*rāst.hamār*) and protector of the Bridge (*pūhlpān*),[127] it becomes a broad bridge (for) the righteous, as much as the height (i.e. to the extent) of nine spears (*nēzak*)—and the length of those which they carry is each separately three arrows (*nāδ*)[128]; and it becomes a narrow bridge (for) the wicked, even unto the semblance of the edge (*tāy*) of a razor.[129]

(6) And that (i.e. the soul) of the righteous passes over the bridge,[130]—

and the pleasantness of the path is compared to the joy one feels when amidst the fragrant winds on a fair morn of spring.

(7) But that of the wicked, as it takes a step forward on the Bridge, falls from the middle of the Bridge on account of exhaustion (*siparīh*)[131] and the sharpness (of the edge), and rolls over (*gartēt*) headlong,[132]—

and the unpleasantness of his path to Hell is compared to the suffering of one walking upon ground studded with sharp points and amidst foul and sickening stench.[133]

---

[126] Literally, 'place, spot.'

[127] Referring possibly to Srōsh. West takes this sentence with § 4.

[128] The 9 spears of 3 arrows each, in length, make up the 27 arrows mentioned in § 3. See above, IrBd. 30. 1, page 92. Cf. also AVN. 5. 1; according to MX. 2. 123-124, the bridge becomes a 'league' (*frasang*) wide.

[129] Cf. also Dk. 9. 20. 3. Dr. Haas calls my attention to the corresponding simile applied to the narrow path of Yoga in Kaṭha Upanishad 3. 14.

[130] Cf. also DD. 20. 3; 34. 3; 42. 2; 81. 18; 85. 7.

[131] Anklesaria suggests *nēzakvarīh* as a possible emendation, but it does not suit the sense (see ed. Anklesaria, p. 45 n. 28).

[132] Cf. also DD. 20. 4; 25. 6; 34. 4; Handarz i Hōsrav i Kavātān, 5; MX. 21. 19; 40. 31; 41. 12; ŠNŠ. 12. 2.

[133] DD. 21. 2-8.

THE INDIVIDUAL JUDGMENT

Before we close this section, we may note a point or two closely connected with the subject. We are already familiar with the teaching of the Gāthās, according to which Zarathushtra himself shall guide the faithful over the awesome Bridge.[134] No trace of this doctrine is to be found in the extant literature of the Later Avesta, but search has now revealed an allusion to it in the Pahlavi book Vichītakīhā i Zātsparam. The author speaks about the compassionate and cheerful nature of the Prophet, and narrates an incident to illustrate this. Once upon a time Zarathushtra came to a swiftly flowing river which was hard for women and old men to cross. Zarathushtra found seven such individuals, who could not cross the river.

> and they were made to cross by him in the manner of a bridge (*pūhl*). This was a sign (*nīšān*) of the bridge-work (*pūhlīh*) of the (spiritual) performers <that is, he was one who leads (*vitārkar*) to Heaven (*vahišt*)>.[135]

Thus the prophet Zarathushtra is here hinted at, if not explicitly mentioned, as the one who will lead the soul of the faithful on to Paradise across the Chinvat Bridge—the architect of the invisible Bridge that leads from earth to Heaven.

The other point to be mentioned is found in a passage that is unique in Pahlavi literature.[136] Though having no direct relation to the Bridge, it does have a bearing on the lot of the soul. This is an allusion in the Artāk Vīrāz Nāmak to 'a great river, dark as dreadful Hell,' composed of the tears of relatives who indulged in excessive lamentations over the departed.[137]

---

[134] See above, page 58.

[135] VZsp. 20. 5 (= ed. Anklesaria, 14. 2, 3); note a strikingly parallel couplet in Longfellow's Golden Legend, canto 5.

[136] Though the idea is repeated in the later Persian Zoroastrian literature; see below, pages 107–109.

[137] It may be observed that this narrative is not quite consistent with the doctrine of the strict accounting at the Bridge, since the soul is made to suffer at another place and for an offense which others have committed. This and other narratives in the Artāk Vīrāz Nāmak and elsewhere in the Iranian literature are allegorical and need not be taken too literally.

The saint Vīrāz, seeing a multitude of distressed souls in this river (*andar an rūt*), some unable to cross, some crossing only with great difficulty, while others cross easily, asks Srōsh the righteous and Ātar the angel about the cause of their misery. He learns:—

(7) This river is the many tears which men shed from the eyes (*čašm*) as they make lamentation and weeping for the departed.
(8) They pour forth those tears unlawfully (*adātīhā*), and these are added (*awzāēt*) to this river.
(9) They who are unable to cross over are those for whom, after their departure, much lamentation and weeping were made; (10) but they (who cross) more easily are those for whom less (lamentation and weeping) were made.[138]

The river must have caused suffering not only to the wicked souls, just before reaching Hell, but to pious souls as well, while they were on their way to Heaven, although nothing is mentioned explicitly on the subject. Evidently the writer's object in introducing the 'river of tears' [139] is to express his disapproval of the then prevailing custom of loud lamentation. Excessive mourning for the departed has always been considered by Zoroastrians as a sin,[140] being injurious to the bodily and mental health of the mourners, besides causing distress to the soul of the departed.

Conclusion. The evidence deduced from the Pahlavi books in connection with the Individual Judgment is sufficient to show that in these writings we find a fuller elaboration of ideas that are more briefly presented in the older literature. This is par-

[138] AVN. 16. 7–10. The New Persian metrical version of Zaratusht Bahrām gives a more detailed description of the river; see below, page 108.

[139] Somewhat distantly related is the idea of a dread river to be crossed by souls, e.g. the Styx in Greek mythology, the Vaitaraṇī of the Hindus, the Gyöll of the Scandinavians.

[140] Cf. Dk. 9. 17, 4.

ticularly noticeable in regard to the doctrines concerning a spiritual store of merits and demerits accruing from one's thoughts, words, and deeds, and the accounting and reckoning, or auditing and balancing at the heavenly tribunal, presided over by the three Judges, Mihr, Srōsh, and Rashnū, whose names are mentioned several times. The Bridge of Judgment and its crossing by the soul are depicted in greater detail. Much of the information contained in these Pahlavi writings reappears in the later Parsi-Persian literature, as will be indicated in the following chapter.

CHAPTER X

THE INDIVIDUAL JUDGMENT ACCORDING TO THE PARSI-PERSIAN LITERATURE

Introduction. The allusions to the Individual Judgment in the later Persian Zoroastrian literature serve as a supplement to the teachings of the Pahlavi books. Though to a large extent they are mere repetitions of the ideas already presented, they occasionally offer some slight additional material. Therefore, although it is not necessary to cite them in full, a number of the more significant passages are here selected.

The store of Good Works, and related ideas. As in the Avesta and Pahlavi accounts, the later Persian writings lay great emphasis on the constant performance of 'duties and good works' (*kār u karfa*), so that these may come to the succor of the doers at the Chinvat Bridge. These meritorious actions, which are stored up in the treasure-house of Heaven, can secure for the soul a safe passage over the Bridge of Judgment.

Among the numerous acts of merit, steadfastness in the religion and helping others also to be steadfast is the best, and leads one's soul to Heaven,[1]

> and we know that the arrival in Heaven (*bahišt*) shall be through virtuous actions (*kardār i nīk*), and through them we shall obtain salvation (*rastagārī*); and we think of good (*nīkī andīšīm*), speak of good (*nīkī gūyīm*), and do good (*nīkī kunīm*).[2]

The faithful should not postpone today's duties and good works till tomorrow. The archfiend, Aharman, has specially appointed two of his assistants to the foul work of deceiving

---
[1] SD. 60. 1–2, 4–5, text ed. Dhabhar, p. 42; cf. transl. West, *SBE*. 24. 321–322.
[2] SD. 60. 3. Cf. transl. West, *SBE*. 24. 321; text ed. Dhabhar, p. 42.

mankind, so that their duties and good works are delayed and postponed. The names of these fiends are Tardy (*dīr*) and By-and-by (*pas*),[3] because—

> as to every duty and good work that comes forward, that fiend whose name is Tardy speaks thus: 'Thou wilt live long, and this duty can be done at any time (lit. at all times)'; and that fiend whose name is By-and-by says: 'Since it can be performed afterwards, abandon it for the present.'[4]

And these two fiends united keep the soul away from its own duty till the day of death. It is thus deprived of the benefit arising from the performance of duties and good works.[5]

The idea of the 'Place of Perpetual Profit,' already embodied in the doctrine of the Pahlavi period (see above, p. 74), is clearly set forth in the Parsi-Persian writings, notably in the Sad Dar and the Sad Dar Bundahish. They expressly mention this region as the 'Treasury of Perpetual Profit' (*ganj i hamīša sūd*), where the works of supererogation are stored up for the purpose of granting them to souls who deserve them but have been unable to acquire a sufficiency.[5a]

The Sad Dar furthermore states that the celebration of the six[6] important ceremonies, with which we are already familiar through the Pahlavi treatise Shāyist nē-Shāyist,[7] redounds to great merit. If one neglects to perform these or order these to be performed, he commits what is termed a 'bridge-sin'

---

[3] SD. 81. 1, 13–15; cf. the Avestan *Būšyqstā*, the longhanded demoness of sleepiness, see Vd. 18. 16.

[4] SD. 81. 16. Cf. transl. West, *op. cit.* p. 347; text ed. Dhabhar, p. 58.

[5] SD. 81. 17–18; cf. also SDBd. 28. 1–7 (ed. Dhabhar, p. 96–97); PhlRiv. 28 (ed. Dhabhar, p. 95–97), cf. above, page 74.

[5a] See SD. 64. 9 (cf. West in *SBE.* 24. 327 n. 6), and SDBd. 65. 5 (ed. Dhabhar, p. 136). Cf. also SD. 1. 5, see below, page 102.

[6] The Sad Dar makes the number six (instead of five, as in the Pahlavi) since it separates the celebration of the ceremonies performed in honor of the sun and moon into two.

[7] Cf. ŠNŠ. 12. 31; see above, page 79.

(*gunāh i pūl*), and for this he undergoes severe punishment (*pādfrāh*) at the Chinvat Bridge.[8]

Closely connected with the subject of merit and sin is the doctrine of repentance (*patit*), often mentioned in these Persian writings. We are told that repentance must be made for every sin. When one repents of sins committed, he undergoes some punishment at the Bridge, but escapes the tortures of Hell. And this repentance is not a mere penance, but requires a complete change of heart and will, a sincere renunciation of that sin for the future; otherwise it is useless.[9]

There is one particular class of sins which receive special mention in the Persian Rivāyats and with which we are already familiar.[10] These are the *hamēmāl* sins, for which there is no retribution (*tōjaš*),

> except when thou beggest forgiveness of that person whom thy sin has injured. If not,[11] then they (i.e. the Judges) detain the soul at the Chinvat Bridge until its adversary arrives and exacts justice from it; then it obtains release (*rahā'ī*),[12]

and is disposed of, in the usual manner, according to the balance of its good and bad actions.

The soul at the Chinvat Bridge. On the dawn of the fourth day after death the soul arrives at the Chinvat Bridge, where it is judged on its life record. We may cite here an important passage from the Persian treatise Sad Dar, which describes the weighing of the soul in the traditional manner, but with a noticeable addition to the possibility of the transference of merit:—

---

[8] SD. 6. 1, 6; cf. also RivDH. (Gujarati vers.), p. 43. The Sad Dar and the other Rivāyats dwell at considerable length on the various kinds of merit and sin, which involve the fate of the soul, but space does not permit us to describe them here.

[9] SD. 45. 1, 10, 11.

[10] See above, page 78.

[11] Thus ms. MU; omitted in other mss. See ed. Dhabhar, p. 33 n. 3.

[12] SD. 42. 3–4, ed. Dhabhar, p. 33; cf. transl. West, *op. cit.* p. 305.

THE INDIVIDUAL JUDGMENT

> When the soul, on the fourth night,[13] arrives at the head (*sar*) of the Chinvat Bridge, the angel Mihr and the angel Rashn make up its account (*ḥisāb*) and reckoning (*šumār*). If the good works it has done be scant in measure (*kam māya*), they (i.e. the Judges) assign to it a like portion (*ham naṣīb*)[14] out of each duty and good work (*kār u karfa*) that the faithful (*behdīnān*)[15] have done in the earth of seven regions, in order that (*tā*) the good works may become more in weight, that the soul may arrive in the shining Heaven (*bahišt*), the abode (*jāīgāh*) of the righteous.[16]

The passage seems to imply that a soul which proved to be deficient in good works at the time of accounting may still have the necessary amount made up by the judges out of the superabundance of the merit of other faithful people. The object here in view is to impress on men the importance of steadfastness in the Faith, for that is the chief of all good works and entitles the faithful soul to its share in the general store of good works.[17]

We are informed, furthermore, that even if a sin is trifling it is not desirable to commit it with the thought that this small quantity 'does not possess harm in the hereafter,'[18] for—

> if the quantity of sin (*gunāh*) be such that the sin is even one filament of the hair of the eyelashes more in weight than the good works are, that person arrives in Hell (*dūzax*). And if the quantity of good works be

---

[13] The Pahlavi accounts say at dawn of the fourth day; see page 82.
[14] That is, such a portion as would make up the deficiency in quantity.
[15] Literally, 'those of the good religion,' i.e. the Zoroastrians. The term, as it is used by the Parsis today, is narrowed down in its application, as referring only to 'the laity,' as contrasted with the term *mūbēdān*, referring to 'the priestly class.'
[16] SD. 1. 4–5; cf. above ŠNŠ. 8. 4, see page 77.
[17] SD. 1. 1, 3, 7.
[18] SD. 2. 1–2.

more, he arrives in the shining Heaven, the abode of the righteous.[19]

The Sad Dar, following the Pahlavi texts, recognizes not only the ceremonial rites to be performed for Srōsh continuously during the three days the soul is believed to be in this world, but it also recognizes the celebration of three Drōn ceremonies [20] at the dawn of the fourth night in connection with the judgment of the soul and its passage over the Chinvat Bridge. The earthly sacrament is symbolical of the events that take place in the other world on this exceedingly solemn occasion.[21] The writer of the Sad Dar brings it out in part:—

> While the priest (*hērbad*) consecrates (*yazad*) the suit of clothes (*Jāma*),[22] they (i.e. the Judges) make up the account and reckoning for the soul. When the priest recites *frasasti Ahurahe Mazdå* [23] and removes the Frasast [24] from this side (*īn jānib*) to that

[19] SD. 2. 3-4.
[20] SD. 87. 2.
[21] Equally symbolical is the *Bōδ Dātan* ceremony performed at the hour.
[22] The 'suit of clothes,' considered to be symbolically appropriate for the soul of the departed, is consecrated during the Artāk Fravart ceremony.
[23] The Avestan words here quoted are from Ys. 8. 1, and the term *frasastay-* (from *sawh-* vb., Skt. *praśasti*), lit. 'glory,' is a technical designation. See next note.
[24] A *drōn*, or ceremonial wafer-bread, is a small, flexible pancake, made of wheat flour and water, with a little melted butter (*ghī*), and baked. The word *frasast* is technically employed by the Parsi priests to designate the sacred cake (*drōn*) which is not marked with the nine superficial cuts (in three rows of three each), symbolical of 'good thoughts, good words, and good deeds.' Haug, West, and Bulsara are not correct in noting that a *frasast* is a *drōn* with the nine cuts. (See Haug, *Essays*, 3d ed., p. 396; West, *SBE*. 24. 352 n. 2; Bulsara, *Aērpatastān and Nīrangastān*, p. 87 n. 13; cf. also Modi, *Religious Ceremonies*, p. 296-297). The term *frasast* as applied to the unmarked sacred cake (*drōn*) seems to have its origin in the association with the first word of the clause quoted, *frasasti Ahurahe Mazdå*, with the recital of which the priest lifts the cake so designated. The number of *drōns* consecrated at each of the Drōn Ceremonies differs according to the importance of the divinity thus honored. For the ceremony in honor of Srōsh six *drōns* are

side (*ān jānib*), the soul passes to (*ba*) the Chinvat Bridge.²⁵

And when it arrives at the Chinvat Bridge from the world, on the fourth night, it goes first to the abode of fire (*ātašgāh*),²⁶ and then with one step it arrives at the star station, with the second step it arrives at the moon station, with the third step it arrives at the sun station, (and) with the fourth step ²⁷ it arrives at the Garōtmān.²⁸

The Sad Dar tells us, furthermore, that if one properly propitiates Srōsh during one's lifetime, the angel protects his soul when he dies, even though there be no one at hand to perform the obligatory ceremonies during the first three days when it is supposed to stay near the body ²⁹; and on the dawn of the fourth day,

he is a helper, with the angel Rashn and the angel

consecrated, whereas for those in honor of Rashnū and Ashtāt, the good Vāy, and Artāk Fravart only four *drōns* are required. Of these six or four *drōns*, half the number are marked with the nine superficial cuts, as noted above. As to the arrangement of these *drōns*, marked and unmarked (*frasast*), and of other ceremonial apparatus at the consecration, see Haug, *op. cit.* p. 408.

²⁵ One more point to be noted in this ceremonial may prove of interest, because it carries out the symbolism still further. The *frasast* in question is placed at the right-hand side of the officiating priest, and before it is moved to the left, he lifts it up three times during the recitation of Ys. 8. 1. This may possibly symbolize the three steps or stages by which the soul of the departed reaches the joys of paradise.

²⁶ Literally, 'the throne of fire,' referring to the stone pedestal for the fire-urn.

²⁷ Thus the better text in ms. MU, which has *ba garōtmān* instead of *ba čīnvad pul*, which West followed in his translation. The discrepancy which West (*SBE.* 24. 352 n. 4) commented upon is therefore removed. We may incidentally observe that the four stages of ascent heavenward here mentioned are often alluded to in the Pahlavi books, but the whole treatment of this subject belongs to Part II.

²⁸ SD. 87. 9-11, ed. Dhabhar, p. 61-62. West's section-divisions differ from those adopted here by the present writer.

²⁹ SD. 58. 1-4; see above.

Mihr,[30] at the Chinvat Bridge, while they make up its account and reckoning, and it goes to its own abode.[31]

The late Rivāyat of Shāhpūr Barūchī has further to tell us that when the soul goes to the Chinvat Bridge and renders its accounting,

> the vigor of the soul at this time is like that of a youth of the age of fifteen.[32]

And now we turn to describe some of the ideas, contained in the late Parsi-Persian writings, which are more closely associated with the subject of the crossing of the Chinvat Bridge.

Passage of the soul over the Chinvat Bridge. The Parsi-Persian texts have not much to say regarding either the location or the description of the Bridge itself. Nor do they have anything to add regarding the actual crossing of the soul over the Bridge beyond what we know from the early literature. But they do speak at some length regarding ceremonies or the like which may help the soul in its passage across the Chinvat Bridge.

The Sad Dar tells us that the proper observance of ceremonies in honor of the Fravashis[33] during the last ten days of the year causes the soul of the faithful one, when he passes away, to be welcomed in Heaven by the souls[34] of those who have died previously:—

> And, when he passes away[35] from this world, those souls (i.e. the propitiated spirits) come back to greet

---

[30] Thus the Dhabhar text. Some mss. omit 'and the angel Mihr.' See West, *SBE.* 24. 319.

[31] SD. 58. 5; cf. SDBd. 99. 2 (ed. Dhabhar, p. 168); RivDH. vol. 1, p. 148 (= Gujarati vers. p. 347–348).

[32] RivDH. vol. 1, p. 147 (= Gujarati vers. p. 346); see above, page 20.

[33] Technically known among the Parsis as the *Fravartīkān* ceremonies. For a description of these, see Modi, *Religious Ceremonies*, p. 465–479.

[34] According to this treatise and other later writings, the souls of the departed, and not their Fravashis alone, visit the earth during those ten days, and hence the reception.

[35] Literally, 'they pass away.'

and gladden him (i.e. at the Bridge); and they encourage and praise (*āzādī kunand*) him also in the presence of the creator Ōrmazd, and speak thus: 'The righteous soul did not forget us while he was in the world, and we have been satisfied with him; now we are unanimous (*hamdāstānīm*) that Thou shouldest provide him with an equal share (*ham bahra*) of those good works of ours,[36] and make his soul attain to the abode of the righteous.'

They utter these words, and give that soul confidence (*ōmīd*), while they (i.e. the Judges) make up his account.

Afterwards, with him, they make the passage over the Chinvat Bridge, till he arrives at his own abode, and then they return.[37]

On the contrary, if the person has neglected to honor the Fravashis of the departed relatives in his life-time, they visit his soul with retribution hereafter, because they are dissatisfied:—

For if they return dissatisfied, they utter a curse (*nifrīn*). When the soul departs from this world, they reproach him, and speak thus: 'Thou hadst thought that they (i.e. the Fravashis) united (*payvasta*) will release thee there (i.e. at the Chinvat Bridge). It is not proper for thee to come into this world (i.e. into Heaven).

Now, hadst thou performed duty and good works and hadst thou recollected us, we would have come to thy rescue (*faryād*), and would have released thee from this fearful dwelling-place (i.e. from Hell).'

He experiences much repentance, but obtains no benefit therefrom.[38]

[36] Cf. page 75, above.
[37] SD. 37. 6-8; cf. SDBd. 51, 52 (ed. Dhabhar, p. 123-126).
[38] SD. 37. 10-12.

The Sad Dar informs us that the Barshnūm, or the highest form of ceremonial purification, should be undergone by all, men and women alike.[39] And if one dies without performing the ceremony,

> when the soul arrives at the head of the Chinvat Bridge, the archangels and the angels flee (*gurīzand*) from the stench (*gand*) of that soul, and are not able to make up its account and reckoning. It remains at the Chinvat Bridge and is not able to pass; it becomes very repentant, but gains no benefit (*sūd*) thereby.[40]

The repentance comes too late to exercise a favorable influence on the soul's destiny. Thus the crossing of the Bridge is seriously impeded by the omission of this important ceremonial.

The idea of the dogs that guard the Chinvat Bridge appears likewise in the Sad Dar. We are told that all dogs must be fed and well treated, because not only do they protect men, cattle, and sheep from thieves and wild beasts—their bark driving away the demons and fiends—, but their representatives 'will come at the Chinvat Bridge to the assistance of the soul of those' who have been kind to them.[41]

The Sad Dar mentions also the river of tears, with which we are already familiar.[42] It follows closely the account given in the Pahlavi Artāk Vīrāz Nāmak.[43] The relatives and friends

---

[39] SD. 36. 1–3. The ceremony was originally intended only for those who became unclean through any serious defilement (see Vd. 8. 35–72; 9. 1–57; 19. 20–25). The original object was widened, and as a measure of precaution all were enjoined to undergo this purificatory ceremony. But at present this *Barəšnūm* ceremony is undergone generally by members of the priestly class, so as to qualify them for some higher religious ceremonies, and in rare cases by the male members of the laity for the *tan pāk*, or the purification of the body. The ceremony takes its designation from the Av. word *barəšnav-*, 'head,' as in Vd. 8. 40, 41, the first part of the body to be washed. For a description of the ceremony see Modi, *Religious Ceremonies*, p. 102–153.

[40] SD. 36. 5–6.
[41] SD. 31. 1–6.
[42] See above, page 96.
[43] AVN. 16.

of the departed are not to give way to excessive lamentation and weeping,

> because every tear (that) issues (from) the eye goes to that river before the Chinvat Bridge, and then the soul of the deceased remains at that place, and it is difficult for it to make the passage; it is not able to pass over the Chinvat Bridge.[44]

It is therefore incumbent upon the surviving relatives and friends, instead of mourning and causing suffering to the departed, to recite the prayers for the dead and perform the necessary ceremonials—

> so that the passage of that place may become easy (*āsān*) for it.[45]

Among the versions of the Artāk Vīrāz Nāmak in Persian verse, the principal one is that made by Dastur Zaratusht Bahrām.[46] This describes the river of tears in greater detail than does the Pahlavi book. The river is not only dark and gloomy (*sīyāh u tār*), but a feature is added that it emitted the most pestilential vapors (*ganda*). There were to be seen upon it a vast number of souls, all in the agony of drowning. Many of these were sinking, and every one of them seemed to be in the greatest distress (*ranj*). They were calling on Ōrmazd, and were asking for forgiveness, that they might be relieved of their misery. The saint was deeply touched by this gloomy spectacle, and felt pity for the sufferings of the unhappy souls. Thereupon he inquired of his spiritual guide, the angel Srōsh,

---
[44] SD. 96. 2.
[45] SD. 96. 3.
[46] See Haug and West, *The Book of Arda Viraf*, introd. p. 19. The Persian metrical version was composed in A.Y. 900 (A.D. 1530–1531) from an anonymous prose version, edited for the first time by Dastur Kaekhusru Dastur Jamaspaji in his *Arda Viraf Nameh*, Bombay, 1902. For the translation see J. A. Pope, *The Ardai Viraf Nameh, or the Revelations of Ardai Viraf, translated from the Persian and Guzeratee versions*, London, 1816.

as to who the souls were that endured such punishment.[47] The rest of the account is similar to what we find in the original Pahlavi book.

In connection with the Chinvat Bridge, the Sad Dar has an allusion which shows the importance of marrying early, so as to benefit by the good works of one's children.[48] The writer goes on to tell us that the very word *pūr* ('son') has the connotation of 'bridge' (*pūl*), because by this bridge they pass into the other world [49]; and furthermore,

> if a person has no child, they call him 'one with a severed bridge' (*burīda pūl*), that is, the way for him to the other (lit., that) world is severed, and he is not able to arrive in that world.
>
> At the head of the Chinvat Bridge he shall remain; even if he has performed many deeds of duty and good works, he is not able to make a passage over the Chinvat Bridge, and they (i.e. the Judges) do not make up his account and reckoning.[50]

And therefore a childless man must have an adopted son. If a person dies without having a son of his own or an adopted son, it is a duty incumbent upon the relatives of the dead to appoint an adopted son for him; and if they fail to do so, they in turn will be barred from passing over the Bridge until they have made amends to the wronged soul.[51]

The same idea occurs in the Persian version of the Artāk

[47] See Dastur Kaekhusru's ed., p. 19–20, and Pope's translation, p. 54. The Rivāyat of Kāmā Bahrā also mentions 'the river of tears' and quotes both the Sad Dar and Zaratusht Bahrām's account, just quoted. See RivDH. (Gujarati vers.), p. 340–343.

[48] SD. 18. 1–3; cf. ṢNṢ. 10. 22; 12. 15; SDBd. 29 (ed. Dhabhar, p. 97–98).

[49] SD. 18. 4. As West points out, this fanciful explanation must be derived from a Pahlavi source, as it is only in that language that the two words ($p\ n\ r$) are written alike.

[50] SD. 18. 5–6.

[51] SD. 18. 10–19; cf. SDBd. 62 (ed. Dhabhar, p. 134). See Modi, *Religious Ceremonies*, p. 82–83, 440.

Vīrāz Nāmak made by Zaratusht Bahrām, though it is not to be found in the original Pahlavi text. The Persian version narrates how Saint Vīrāz comes to the Chinvat Bridge after visiting both Heaven and Hell, and is carried by his celestial guides into a desert.[52] Here he saw many souls that were not able to pass the bridge, but wandered up and down, confounded and distressed. They came to the saint and spoke to him of their unhappy lot because of not having a child, natural or adopted, and begged of Vīrāz to carry their message to the world of the living, that no man should die without leaving an heir.[53]

Though this idea is not explicitly mentioned in the extant Avesta and Pahlavi writings, it may nevertheless be old in Zoroastrianism. We may possibly gather this from certain passages in the Avesta, where the devout worshiper prays to Mazdāh for the boon of *frazaintūm azō.būjim,* 'child, relieving from distress,' which the Pahlavi translation renders by *hač tangīh bōxtārīh,* with the gloss *hač dōzax^v,* 'from Hell.'[54]

Search has now revealed an Avestan fragment which bears directly on the subject. This fragment is preserved in the Pahlavi treatise **Vicharkart i Dēnīk**, and runs as follows:—

> If the dead man be childless, then one shall give him a son (i.e. shall adopt a son for him), O Spitama Zarathushtra, in order that the son may support him across the Chinvat Bridge (*puθrō haom urvānəm činvat̰.pərətūm vīδārayat̰*).[55]

[52] See AVN. 53. 2.
[53] See Pope's translation, p. 95. Both the SD. account and this narrative are quoted by RivDH. (Gujarati vers.), p. 356–359.
[54] Cf. Ys. 62. 5; Yt. 13. 134; see Bthl. *AirWb.* 362. The Hindus have a similar conception on the subject of the appointment of an heir. The Sanskrit word *putra* is assigned a popular etymology in the Brahmanical writings (e.g. Yāska, Nirukta 2. 11) as composed of *put,* 'hell,' and *tra,* 'delivering,' from the idea that a son saves from Hell; cf. also Manusmṛti 9. 138.
[55] See Vicharkart i Dēnīk, Frag. 2 and 4 (= Bthl. *IF.* 12. 94–95); cf. also Frag. 17 (= *ibid.* p. 100), which refers to the injunction about the adoption of a son on the third day after death.

This Avestan fragment is stated to be from the old Hadhōkht Nask. The statement may be correct so far as the content of the text is concerned, but its grammatical structure and style in general show signs of lateness.[56]

Conclusion. It will be seen from the material presented that the Parsi-Persian literature amplifies a number of points contained in the earlier religious writings of the Parsis regarding an Individual Judgment. The store of Good Works is to be replenished especially by performing, or more frequently by ordering to be performed, ceremonies of one kind or another. The evidence is sufficient to show that the doctrine concerning the account and reckoning at the Chinvat Bridge by the divine triad of Judges, and regarding the crossing of the Bridge, continued to be a recognized tenet in the Zoroastrian Doctrine of a Future Life.

[56] See also Bthl. *IF*. 12. 93 n. 2.

CHAPTER XI

CONCLUSION

> 'And then may we be those who will make this world perfect!'
> —Ahunavaitī Gāthā, Ys. 30. 9.

Step by step we have traced the fate of the soul from death to the individual judgment where its lot, for weal or woe, is assigned. The experiences of the disembodied spirit during the first three nights, joyous or sorrowful according as its life in this world has been righteous or wicked, have been narrated according to the texts. The ordeal which each must undergo in the assize over which stern judges preside is a test filled with awe for just and unjust alike. This is the accounting at which all life's records are impartially weighed in the balance before the soul can attempt to cross the Chinvat Bridge, that span over which all must go. The images associated with the passage of this 'Bridge of the Separator' cannot fail to impress the imagination, while at the same time they recall parallels to be found in other religions.[1]

At this point in the drama of the soul's destiny our investigation must be halted for the present, but it may be serviceable to add an outline of the remaining doctrine concerning the future life, inasmuch as allusions have incidentally been made to it in the foregoing chapters, and also for the sake of indicating the proportions of the subject as a whole.

The fateful crossing of the Bridge means either joy or doom. The ascent to felicity rises through the past accumulation of good thoughts (*humata*), good words (*hūxta*), and good deeds (*hvaršta*) into the beatitude of Garō-demāna, 'House of Song.' It is natural that the Zoroastrian texts should descant on the

---
[1] Cf. above, page 49, note 1*a*.

grades that lead to Heaven, the abode of joys pure in their spirituality, the realm where the Best Thought (*Vahišta Manah*) dwells.

The *descensus Averno* in the Zoroastrian texts matches in inverse order the path upward. Through its own evil thoughts (*dušmata*), evil words (*dužuxta*), and evil deeds (*dužvaršta*), the soul of the damned sinks lower and lower to Hell, until it falls into the dark abyss of Drujō-demāna, 'House of the Fiend.' Suffering anguish and crying words of woe, the wicked soul is plunged into still greater terror and misery to be endured for ages to come.

There is also in Zoroastrianism the doctrine of an intermediate state, the tenet of Hamistakān, or 'Equilibrium.' Zarathushtra recognized the possibility that the good and evil deeds of an individual might balance exactly when weighed in the scales at the heavenly tribunal; and a special place and condition are assigned to such a soul until its ultimate fate shall have been determined at the Universal Judgment.

Zarathushtra's keen vision and logical mind caught glimpses of this General Judgment at the end of all things. This optimistic hope of the dawn of a new and better eon is the note that rings again and again in the Gāthās. The Prophet's graphic presentation of these events may well have stirred the imagination of his hearers and inspired his followers to carry on the task of furthering the Wished-for Kingdom (*xšaθra vairya*) and to look forward to the day when good shall finally triumph over evil. The righteous shall be divided from the wicked at the great Separation (*vīdāiti*), when the flood of molten metal (*ayah xšusta*) shall institute the ordeal which all must ultimately undergo, and the world shall be restored to perfection (*frašōkərəti*).

The accounts given in the Later Avestan and Pahlavi books are essentially the same as those found in the Gāthās, except that the picturesque side is more fully developed. Among these younger portions of the Zoroastrian Scriptures, the old stanzas of the Zam Yazat Yasht (Yt. 19. 89-96) elaborately develop

CONCLUSION

the Gāthic doctrine of the Last Things. Fortunately, too, there survives in the well-known Pahlavi book Bundahishn, doubtless drawn from the Dāmdāt Nask of the original Avesta, a most vivid description of the last days of the world, the coming of the final Saoshyant, the resurrection and general judgment, the decisive conflict between the powers of good and evil, the utter annihilation of evil, the establishment of the kingdom of righteousness, and the reign of good forever and evermore.

Frazaft pa drūt šātīh u rāmišn,
'Completed in welfare, joy, and pleasure.'

INDEXES

I. INDEX OF PASSAGES TRANSLATED

[The Index lists only the principal passages translated. Passages translated only in parts and embodied in the continuous English text have not been listed below, nor has it been possible to incorporate in the present Index the numerous passages referred to throughout the book.]

THE GĀTHĀS

	Page		Page
Ys. 31. 14	49	48. 4	32
31. 20	30	48. 8 c, d	54
32. 15	56	49. 4	51
32. 6	52	49. 5	30
33. 1	50, 57	49. 10	51
34. 2	52	49. 11	31
45. 8	51–52	50. 2 c, d	54
46. 10	58	50. 4	54–55
46. 11	31, 59	51. 13	31, 55
46. 17 c, d	57		

THE LATER AVESTA

	Page		Page
HN. 2. (= Yt. 22). 1–6	10–11	19. 29	38
2. 7–14	33–35	19. 30	36, 38
2. 14b	61	VičDēn. Frag. 2	110
2. 19–24	21–22	Vr. 15. 1	61–62
2. 25–26	37	Ys. 55. 4	60
Vd. 7. 52	69	57. 2	67
13. 8, 9	70	Yt. 10. 32	61
19. 27–30	62–66		

THE PAHLAVI LITERATURE

	Page		Page
AVN. 5. 2–3, 5	85	25. 5	87
6. 9–11	90–91	26. 3	75–76
16. 7–10	97	31. 11	90
17. 10–26	41–43	37. 24	76
DD. 14. 2–5	89–90	38. 3	76
16. 4	25	IrBd. 30. 1	92
16. 7	17	30. 2	12–13
21. 2–7	94–95	30. 3	13–14, 24–25
24. 4	15	30. 4	40
24. 5	86–87	30. 5	40–41
25. 4	24	30. 6	41

118   INDEX OF PASSAGES TRANSLATED

	Page		Page
30. 9–10.	92–93	12. 13–15	90
MX. 2. 96, 97	72	PhlVd. 19. 36	75
2. 115–122	84	ŠVV. 4. 91–96	87–88
2. 161–163	84–85	VZsp. 20. 5	96

THE PARSI-PERSIAN WRITINGS

RivDH. vol. 1, p. 147	20, 105	60. 3	99
vol. 1, p. 148	19–20	81. 16	100
SD. 1. 4–5	102	87. 9–11	103–104
2. 3–4	102–103	96. 2	108
18. 5–6	109	96. 3	108
36. 5–6	107	SDBd. 24. 4–5	26–27
37. 6–8	105–106	99. 1	18
37. 10–12	106	99. 5–9	44–45
42. 3–4	101	99. 15–20	45
58. 5	104–105		

II. INDEX OF PAHLAVI WORDS

[The index lists only those words which are quoted from the texts translated by the author or adduced in the footnotes and printed in *italics* in accordance with the system adopted and explained on page xiv. The numbers refer to the pages.]

adātihā 97
aδāv 13
afsūs 35
ahrāmēt 88
akāmakīhā 93
an 97
andar 86, 97
angušt 94
an-š 73, 87
artāk fravart 86
arzūr grīvak 80
asar rōšnīh 76
ašātīh 17
āškārak 84
āšnāk 64
atōxt 87
awāj-kūn 42
awzāēt 97
āyāft 86
ayāwār 88
āzarm 84
azem 25

bālist 92
bāmīk 63, 86
band 15, 63, 84
banjišn 16
barəšnūm 107
bārīk 94
bē 24, 77
béš 15
bōδ 17, 64
bōjēt 88
bōstān 40

bōxtan 25
bōxtārīh 110
būn 15, 74
burīnēt 93

čahārom 86
čandīh 89
čarāitīk 43, 87
čašm 97
čikāt i dāitīk 79, 82, 92, 94
čīnīt 86
činvat pūhl 55

dahēt 93
dānk (mad) 91
dār 94
dārēt 14, 84
darītak 23
darvandīh 85
dātəstān 84
dēhəpatān 84
dēn 44
dēr 43
dirham 91
dit 40
dōbārišn 24
dōš 74
dōžax^v 90, 110
drafšnīk 43
drōn 86, 103
druj 76
duš-gōnak 42
dušmat 93
dužuxt 93
dužvaršt 93

119

INDEX TO PAHLAVI WORDS

dušxᵛārīh 15

ēstēnd 83
ēstēt 15
ēvak 41
ēvīnak 9

frāj-jānū 42
frasang 91, 95
frasast 103
fravartūkān 79, 105
fröhar 9

ganj 51, 76, 77
ganjbar 73, 86
ganjbarān 87
gartēt 95
gās 14
gāsānbār 78
gāv 40
gēhīkīh 89
gōbišn 77
gūk 92, 93
gyāk 95

hač 40, 110
hamah 40
hamār 14, 40, 74, 81, 90
hamārōmand 87
hamārīhēt 81
hamārkar 89
hamārkarān 88, 90
hamawrank 13
hamēmār 78
hamēmārān 89
hamēšak sūt gāh 74, 75
hamistakān 74
hamkārān 12
hamxᵛēšīh 88
hanākīh 17
hanbār 72, 73, 74, 75, 86, 87
handāč 12
handāčēt 85
hangrād 84
harburz 79
hōm 25

hūbaxtak 89
hūčihr 40, 86
hūgōvišnīh 24
hūkūnišnīh 24
hūmat 93
hūmēnišnīh 24
hūxt 93
hvaršt 93

i 14, 17, 23, etc

jān 9, 17
jēh 42

kanīk 39, 40, 86
karīnišn 13
karp 94
karpak 72, 74, 81, 86, 90
kārt 93
kōstak 40
kūnēt 84, 90

mēnūk 24
mēnūkān 83
mīyānčīkīh 83

nāδ 91, 94, 95
nē 84, 93
nēwak(nēk) 13
nēzak 91, 92, 95
nīšān 96
nīyāzakīhā 95
nyāᵛišn 21

ō 13, 89
ōftēt 63
ōšahīn 85
ōstarak 91, 94

pa 15, 21, 85, 89
pāδ 94
padvaxtag 68
pāhlūk 94
pasāxt 17
pāt 73
pātdahišn 76

INDEX OF PAHLAVI WORDS

pātfrās 15
patūtīh 76, 77, 78
patmān 89
pīš 40
pūhl 94, 96
pūhlīh 96
pūhlpān 95
pūr-āp 40
pūr-bar 40
pūr-mīvak 40
pūr-patixū 40
pušt 94
pūtak 23

rāmišn 15
rapiθwin 79
rāstihā 81, 90
rāst.hamār 95
ravēt 13
rūt 97
ruvān 9, 16, 81
ruvānīk 78

sahēt 41
sak 92
sāmān 89
šap 12
šapšēr 91, 92
sar 92, 93.
šātihēt 40
sērīh 83
setōš 73, 74, 79, 82, 89, 90
siparīh 95
škaft 81
šnāsak 30
spēt 14
srōš 68
srōšō.čaranām 90, 91
sūkīhā 94
sūt 75

tāk 75
tākīh 89
tan 9, 13, 16, 17
tan i pasīn 17, 89
tang 94

tangīh 110
tapēt 13
tarāzīnītarīh 83
tarāzūk 74, 81, 83, 85
tāy 91, 92, 93, 94, 95
tēž 91, 92, 93, 94
tiγr 93
tōčišn 15, 77

u 23, 74, 90
uš 63
ušbāmīk 63

vāč 86
vahišt 90, 96
var 94
var nīrang 68
vas 12, 94
vastrak 14, 23
vāt 13
vattar 84
vaxš 74
vāy i vattar 83
vāy i vēh 83
vičārišnōmand 36
vičāšišnīh 63
vīmārəstān 88
vinās 73, 81, 87, 90
višōpišn 13, 17
vitarg 93
vitārkar 96

wišātak (= *vi°*) 42

xōn 13
xrōštag 68
xup 30
xᵛatāyān 84
xᵛēšak 86
xᵛēš.kārīh 89

zamān 43
zan 42
zarrēn 85
zart 85
zīšttar 42

III. GENERAL INDEX

A

Abode of Good Thought, 50, 56
account of merits and demerits, 49–53, 60–62, 72–77, 99–100
    balancing of the, 57, 62, 66, 81–85, 102–103
Achaemenian kings, future life not mentioned in inscriptions of, 3
Aēshma (Ēshm), demon, 12, 83
Ahriman, see 'Angra Mainyu'
Ahura Mazdāh, account of deeds kept by, 52, 60, 90
    as Separator at the Chinvat Bridge, 56–57, 59
    meritorious deeds treasured by, 51
    past merits shown to the soul by, 61
    souls in the river of tears call upon, 108
Ahuras (Amesha Spentas), 52 n. 20, 56
Alburz, mountain, see 'Harā'
Angra Mainyu (Ahriman), 19, 42, 51 n. 14, 69, 99
Aredvī Sūrā, 34 n. 8, 36 n. 22
Ārmaiti, 30, 65 n. 31
Arnobius, quoted, 16
Artāk Fravart ceremony, 86, 103 n. 22
Artāk Vīrāz, saint, 14, 23, 85, 97, 108, 110
Artāk Vīrāz Nāmak, 14, 23, 39, 41–43, 85, 90–91, 96–97, 107, 108–109, 110
Asha Vahishta, 30, 31, 52, 54, 55, 57, 60
Ashtāt, angel, 85, 86, 103 n. 24
Astō-vīdhātu (Astvidāt), demon, 12, 23, 83
Ātar, angel, 14, 23, 85, 97
Ātash-varahrām fire, the, 13

B

Bāj ceremonies, 86 n. 74
balance, deeds weighed in the, 54, 57, 81, 83, 85, 101–102, cf. 74
    held by Rashnu, 57, 85
balancing of the life account, 57, 61, 62, 66, 81–85, 89–90, 102–103
Barshnūm ceremony, 107
Bartholomae, C., quoted, 28
Behistan inscription of Darius, quoted, 3 n. 2
Bendva, followers of, 51 n. 9
body, the soul hovers near the, 10–14, 17, 18, 21–22
    the soul hopes to re-enter the, 13, 25
Bridge of Judgment, see 'Chinvat Bridge'
Bundahishn, Indian, 15, 24, 82
    Iranian, 12–14, 15, 24–25, 40–41, 43, 44 n. 23, 91–93

C

ceremonies, Drōn, 42, 86, 103
    five indispensable, 78, 79, 100–101
    helpful to the departed soul, 108
    in honor of the Fravashis, 105–106
    in honor of Srōsh, 16, 19, 20, 26, 73 n. 5, 103, 104
    symbolism in, 103, 104
ceremony, the Barshnūm, 107
    the Yazishn, 42
    the Zinda-ravān, 18
Chikāt i Dāitīk, 79 n. 37, 82, 92–94
child, importance of having a, 109–110
Chinvat Bridge, 11, 14, 15 n. 28, 22, 31, 36, 38, 44, 45, 69–70, 99, 109, 110

122

GENERAL INDEX

explanation of the name, 55 n. 42
judgment at the, 53–59, 62–68, 80–91, 101–105
location of the, 79–80
Manichaeism possibly preserves idea of the, 91 n. 107
parallels to the, in other religions, 49 n. 1a
passage of the soul over the, 91–96, 105–107
varying width of the, 92, 94–95
Conscience (daēnā), 28, 29
 manifestation of the, to the soul, 28–45, 73, 93
consciousness (baoδah, bōδ), 17, 33 n. 1, 64
courtesan, the Daēnā of the wicked appears in the guise of a, 43

D

Daēnā, discussion of the term, 28, 29
 manifestation of the, to the soul, 28–45, 73, 93, cf. 86–87
Dāitīk, river, 80
Damāvand, Mount, possible location of the Chinvat Bridge, 80
Dātastān i Dēnīk, 14–15, 16–17, 23–24, 25, 40, 43, 73–74, 75–76, 82 n. 50, 86–87, 88–90, 94–95
Dātastān i Mēnūk i Khrat, 23, 39, 41, 72, 82–85, 90
death, state of probation ends at, 25 n. 18
 Zoroastrian definition of, 9 n. 2
deeds, the wicked soul beholds its evil, 23
 weighed in the balance, 54, 57, 81, 83, 85, 101–102, cf. 74
demons, the soul harassed by, 12, 15, 19, 39, 47, 48
Dēnkart, 17, 39–40, 43
Dispensation, the Final, 52 n. 27, 56
dogs, the two, 70, 92 n. 110, 107
 the Maiden accompanied by, 36, 65

Drōn ceremonies, 42, 86, 103, cf. 79 n. 37
 detailed account of the, 103 n. 24

E

ego, the author prefers not to render daēnā by, 28–29
Endless Light, 76
Ēshm (Aēshma), demon, 12, 83
evil deeds, the wicked soul beholds its, 23
evil thoughts, words, and deeds, 24, 30, 31
expiation, 53, 77–78

F

faculties of man, the five spiritual, 9 n. 1, 33 n. 1
Farnbag fire, the, 92
Fihrist, by an-Nadīm, quoted, 46, 47
fire, kept burning for three days, 16
 the Ātash-varahrām, 13
 the Farnbag, 92
Frashōkereti, Final Renovation, 2, 3, 17, 86
Fravartīkān ceremonies, 105 n. 33
Fravashis, ceremonies in honor of the, 105–106
 offerings to the, 86
freedom of the will, 1
Frēhzīsht, demon, 83

G

Garōtman (Garō-demāna), 93, 104, 112 (see also 'House of Song')
Gāthās, the, 4–5, 28–32, 49–59
Geldner, K. F., quoted, 29 n. 5
good thoughts, words, and deeds, 24, 34, 35, 60, 61, 93
good works, the store of, 49–53, 60–62, 72–77, 99–100
 the five indispensable, 78–79
Grehma, opponent of Zarathushtra, 52

GENERAL INDEX

grief, disapproval of excessive, 96–97, 107–108

H

Hadhōkht Nask, 9–11, 21–22, 33–35, 37, 61, 111

hag, the Daēnā appears in the form of a hideous, 33, 37, 41, 42, 45, 48, 73, cf. 87

Hamistakān, 32, 50, 74 n. 9, 90–91, 93 n. 119, 113

Harā (Harburz, Alburz), mountain, 63 n. 19, 36, 66, 79, 82, 92

heaven (Paradise), 34 n. 5, 45, 60 n. 2, 70, 75, 76, 90, 96, 99, 103, 105–106

four stages of ascent to, 104

hell, 37 n. 27, 38, 43, 45, 51 n. 12, 79–80, 88 n. 91, 90–91, 93, 94, 95, 102, 106, 110

dread of, 24

Herodotus, 3 n. 3, 53 n. 31, 81 n. 44

House of Song, 50, 52, 55, 112

House of the Lie (Druj), 31, 50, 59, 113

Huspāram Nask, 78

J

Jackson, Prof. A. V. Williams, ix, 4 n. 5, 9 n. 1, 29, 46–48, 68 n. 42, 69 n. 44, 81 n. 44

Judges, the heavenly, 56–59, 64, 67–68, 82–85, 101–102

Judgment at the Chinvat Bridge, 53–59, 62–68, 80–91, 101–105

Bridge of, see 'Chinvat Bridge'

General, 17 n. 39, 49 n. 1, 55 n. 45, 58, 90 n. 100

Peak of, 79 n. 37, 80, 94 (see also 'Chikāt i Dāitīk')

Seat of, 64 n. 29, 65 n. 33, 66

judicium particulare, 49 n. 1, 54, 72, 79, 82

judicium universale, 49 n. 1, 55 n. 45, 90 n. 100

K

Karpans and Kavis, 31, 56, 59

Khshathra, archangel, 54

Kimā Gāthā, 11 n. 9, 21, 22

L

lamentations of the wicked soul, 27, 70, 85

life, human, has two parts, 53 n. 28

Longfellow, poet, 96 n. 135

M

maiden, the Daēnā appears in the form of a, 33, 34, 39, 40, 44, 47, 64–65, 66, 73, 93, cf. 86

Mānī, 46, 47, 48

Manichaean texts, quoted, 47–48, 68 n. 42, 81 n. 44, 91 n. 107

Manichaeism, allusion to the balance in, 81 n. 44

possible reference to the Chinvat Bridge in, 91 n. 107

the figures that meet the soul in, 46–48

'three gods' at the Judgment in, 68 n. 42

Mazdāh, see 'Ahura Mazdāh'

Mēnūk i Khrat, see 'Dātastān i Mēnūk i Khrat'

merit, 25 n. 18, 26, 27, 40, 49–53, 60–62, 72–77, 99–101

accruing from good works of others, 100, 102

record of, see 'account'

Misvāna Gātu, doctrine of, 74–75

Mithra (Mihr), 61, 63, 85, 86 n. 75, 89, 90

one of the triad of judges, 57, 66–68, 82–83, 102, 105

mourning, disapproval of excessive, 96–97, 107–108

N

Nasu, the fiend, 42 n. 15

Nīrangastān, 73 n. 5, 78

Nīzisht, demon, 83
noose, Vīzaresha tries to ensnare the soul with a, 15, 63, 84

O

Ōharmazd, see 'Ahura Mazdāh'
Old Persian Inscriptions, no mention of future life in the, 3
Ōrmazd, see 'Ahura Mazdāh'
Ōshahīn, period of, 82

P

Pahlavi Rivāyat, 14, 23, 39, 41
panorama of misdeeds, the wicked soul beholds a, 23
Paradise (heaven), 45, 60 n. 2, 70, 75, 76, 90, 96, 99, 103, 105–106
four stages of ascent to, 104
Parsi-Persian writings, 7
paths, two, 11, 64
Peak of Judgment, 79 n. 37, 80, 94 (see also 'Chikāt i Dāitīk')
Place of Perpetual Profit, 74–77, 100
Powers of Good and Evil, conflict of the, 30, 69, 88
probation, death ends the state of, 25 n. 18
purification, importance of ceremonies of, 107

R

Rashnu (Rashnū), 89, 90
holds the balance, 57, 85
one of the triad of judges, 57, 67–68, 82–83, 85, 102, 104
record of merits and demerits, 49–53, 60–62, 72–77, 99–100
remission of sins, 53, 77
Renovation, the Final (Frashōkereti), 2, 3, 17, 86
repentance, 25, 53, 77–78, 101, 107
Resurrection, the, 17, 27
retribution, 27
the first, 15

righteous soul, assumed to have some faults, 15 n. 29
clothed in white raiment, 14
experiences of the, during the first three nights, 9–20
Rivāyat of Dārāb Hormazdyār, 8
Rivāyat of Kāmā Bahrā, 19–20, 27 n. 21, 109 n. 47
Rivāyat of Shāhpūr Barūchī, 20, 105
Rivāyats, Parsi-Persian, 8, 19, 101

S

Sad Dar, 8, 18, 99–100, 101–108, 109
Sad Dar Bundahish, 8, 18, 20, 26–27, 44–45, 100
Seat of Judgment, 64 n. 29, 65 n. 33, 66
Separator at the Chinvat Bridge, 56–57, 59
Shāyist nē-Shāyist, 77, 78–79, 90 n. 104, 100
Shkand-vimānīk Vichār, 40, 43, 87–88
silver cord, severed at death, 63
sins, confession of, 77–78
remission of, 53, 77
two classes of, 78, 101
son, importance of having a, 109–110
soul, Avestan term for, 9 n. 1
aware of occurrences, 16
harassed by demons, 12, 15, 19, 39, 47, 48
hovers near the body, 10–14, 17, 18, 21–22
size of the, 20
Spenta Mainyu, 69
Sraosha (Srōsh), angel, 12, 14, 16, 18, 19, 20, 23, 58, 84, 85, 89, 90, 94, 95 n. 127, 97
ceremonies in honor of, 16, 19, 20, 26, 73 n. 5, 86 n. 75, 103, 104
one of the triad of judges, 67–68, 82–83
suffering experienced by the wicked, 22–27, 70
supererogation, works of, 100, 102

Sūtkar Nask, 10 n. 4, 17, 21 n. 3

T

tears, river of, 96–97, 107–109
thesaurus meritorum, 75–76
thread, severed at death, 62
tortures undergone by the sinful, 22–27, 70
treasure-bearers of good and evil deeds, 86–88
Treasure-house of Perpetual Profit, 74–77, 100, cf. 51, 52 n. 21
Turkish Manichaean Fragments, quoted, 47–48, 81 n. 44

U

Ushtavaitī Gāthā, 10, 11, 13 n. 23

V

Vahrām, 83, 85
Vahūman, see 'Vohu Manah'
Vāy (Vayu), the bad, 12, 23, 83
   the good, 83, 85, 86, 92
Vendīdād, see 'Vidēvdāt'
Vicharkart i Dēnīk, 110
Vichītakīhā i Zātsparam, 96
Vidēvdāt, 36–37, 38, 62–66, 69, 70, 75
Vīrāz, Artāk, 14, 23, 85, 97, 108, 110
Vishtāsp Yasht, 11, 89 n. 93
Visprat, 61–62
Vīzaresha (Vīzarsh), demon, 12, 23, 24, 38, 65, 66, 85, 94
   tries to ensnare the soul with a noose, 15, 63, 84

Vohu Manah, archangel, 30, 54 n. 37, 58, 113
   account of deeds taken by, 89, 90

W

weighing of merits and demerits, 57, 81, 83, 85
wicked soul, beholds its sin in retrospect, 23
   described as clothed in rags, 23
   desire of the, to re-enter the body, 13, 25
   lamentations of the, 70, 85
   suffering experienced by the, 22–27, 70
wind, the righteous soul feels a fragrant, 33–34, 40, 44
   the wicked soul meets with a foul-smelling, 37, 41, 43, 45

Y

Yama, Indian god of death, noose of, 63 n. 22
Yasna Haptanghāiti, 5, 30 n. 15
Yazatas, the spiritual, 36, 66, 92
Yazishn ceremony, 42

Z

Zarathushtra, 1, 2, 21, 30 n. 10, 50, 58, 89 n. 93, 96, 113
   as judge, 50, 56, 57
   date of, 4, 5
Zātsparam, Selections of, 96
Zinda-ravān, ceremony, 18
Zrvan, the paths made by, 64